SCHOLASTIC

Teaching Reading With
Cynthia Rylant Books

BY JOAN NOVELLI

NEW YORK • TORONTO • LONDON • AUCKLAND • SYDNEY
MEXICO CITY • NEW DELHI • HONG KONG • BUENOS AIRES

Teaching
Resources

Scholastic Inc. grants teachers permission to photocopy the reproducible pages from this book for classroom use. No other part of this publication may be reproduced in whole or in part, or stored in a retrieval system, or transmitted in any form or by any means, electronic, mechanical, photocopying, recording, or otherwise, without written permission of the publisher. For information regarding permission, write to Scholastic Inc., 557 Broadway, New York, NY 10012.

Edited by Immacula A. Rhodes
Cover and interior design by Kathy Massaro
Interior illustrations by James Graham Hale

ISBN 13: 978-0-439-26276-7
ISBN 10: 0-439-26276-3

Copyright © 2009 by Joan Novelli.
Illustrations © 2009 by Scholastic Inc.
All rights reserved.
Printed in the U.S.A.
Published by Scholastic Inc.

1 2 3 4 5 6 7 8 9 10   40   15 14 13 12 11 10 09

Contents

About This Book

Cynthia Rylant is the acclaimed author of more than 100 books for children, many of them inspired by her life. Her stories invite readers to explore universal themes of feelings, family, and friends—whether in the poetic *When I Was Young in the Mountains* or the playful *Poppleton* series. This book takes a close look at a handful of favorites and provides step-by-step lessons designed to teach comprehension strategies, build word knowledge, explore story elements, and nurture a love of reading and language. Interactive reproducible activity pages feature games, mini-books, and other hands-on materials for extending learning.

What's Inside?

The titles featured in this teaching resource begin with the author's first book, *When I Was Young in the Mountains*, and include other picture books as well as several early-reader series. Here is an overview, along with suggestions for use of the books and activities.

- **Meet Cynthia Rylant (page 6):** Share this author profile and photo to familiarize students with the author. Use the follow-up activity (Reading-Writing Connection, page 6) to encourage students to try out some of the author's story-writing strategies and generate story ideas of their own.

- **Activities to Use With Any Book (pages 7–10):** Extend any lesson with the ideas here, which focus on strengthening essential reading skills.

- **Before Reading:** Each lesson begins with suggestions for introducing the story, encouraging the use of predicting and previewing skills, and activating prior knowledge.

- **During Reading:** This section of each lesson suggests areas of focus for a read-aloud, such as noticing the way pictures support text, figuring out unknown words, making connections to the story, predicting what happens next, and using text features to support fluent reading.

- **After Reading:** Discussion starters invite a closer look at story elements, text features, vocabulary, and more.

- **Extension Activities:** These activities provide support for strengthening reading skills and making connections to other areas of the curriculum.

- **Vocabulary Builder:** From exploring connections among related words to building banks of nouns, verbs, and adjectives and learning how specific word choice sharpens writing, these activities support students in expanding word knowledge.

- **Book Links:** Each lesson also features a list of other books that relate to the learning experience.

Tip

As you read any of the books aloud, model good reading techniques, including reading from left to right and using appropriate phrasing and expression.

- **Reproducible Student Pages:** These engaging, ready-to-use pages include templates, graphic organizers, mini-books, games, and more.

- **Activities for Teaching With More Books by Cynthia Rylant (pages 77–78):** Explore seasons, maps, moons, and more with additional literature-based activities.

- **A Cynthia Rylant Celebration (pages 79–80):** Wrap up an author study with these culminating activities.

Whether you choose to use the featured books and lessons as part of an author study or to share them from time to time as read-alouds, this resource provides the materials you need to enrich students' learning experiences with the inspired and varied literature of Cynthia Rylant.

Resources and References

Armbruster, B. B. and Osborn, M. (2001). *Put reading first: The research building blocks for teaching children to read, kindergarten through grade 3.* Washington, DC: Center for the Improvement of Early Reading Achievement (CIERA).

Beck, I. L., McKeown, M. G., and Kucan, L. (2002). *Bringing words to life: Robust vocabulary instruction.* New York: Guilford Press.

Blevins, W. (2006). *Phonics from A to Z: A practical guide.* New York: Scholastic.

Block, C.C. and Mangieri, J. N. (2004). *Powerful vocabulary for reading success.* New York: Scholastic.

Borland, H. (1979). *Twelve moons of the year.* New York: Knopf.

Collins, K. (1964). *Growing readers.* Portland, ME: Stenhouse.

Fletcher, R. (1993). *What a writer needs.* Portsmouth, NH: Heinemann.

Ray, K. W. (1999). *Wondrous words: Writers and writing in the elementary classroom.* Urbana, IL: NCTE.

Connections to the Standards for Reading and Language Arts

Mid-continent Research for Education and Learning (McREL), a nationally recognized, nonprofit organization, has compiled and evaluated national and state standards, and proposed what teachers should provide for their students to grow proficient in language arts, among other curriculum areas. The activities in this book support these standards for grades K–2 in the following areas.

Reading

- Uses mental images based on pictures and print to aid in comprehension of text

- Uses meaning clues to aid comprehension and make predictions about content

- Uses reading skills and strategies to understand and interpret a variety of literary texts

- Uses reading skills and strategies to understand a variety of familiar literary passages and texts

- Knows setting, main characters, main events, sequence, and problems in stories

- Knows the main ideas or theme of a story

- Relates stories to personal experiences

Writing

- Uses strategies to organize written work

- Uses writing and other methods to describe familiar persons, places, objects, or experiences

- Writes in a variety of forms or genres

- Writes for different purposes

- Uses the stylistic and rhetorical aspects of writing

- Uses descriptive words to convey basic ideas

Source: Kendall, J. S. & Marzano, R. J. (2004). *Content knowledge: A compendium of standards and benchmarks for K–12 education.* Aurora, CO: Mid-continent Research for Education and Learning. Online database: http://www.mcrel.org/standards-benchmarks/

Meet Cynthia Rylant

Born: June 6, 1954, in Hopewell, Virginia

"I grew up in rural West Virginia," says Cynthia Rylant, "and what happened there deeply affects what I write." She recalls a simple, unadorned life—a life without indoor plumbing until she was eight years old, without much money, without picture books, without a local bookstore or even a local library. In fact, Cynthia Rylant never saw the inside of a library until she went away to college.

Still, Cynthia describes her childhood world as "a small sparkling universe that gave me a lifetime's worth of material for my writing." She adds, "I think it was the isolation and insulation of my early years that made me turn inward and just mostly concentrate on what people say, and the things they do in their kitchens and living rooms." Later, Cynthia would think of these small, domestic moments as "life's profound experiences." These are the simple things that recur again and again in her writing: family and friends, beloved pets, deep feelings, and hard-earned wisdom, all fueled by cherished memories of growing up in Appalachia.

Cynthia attended college with the notion of becoming a nurse. But once there, she was introduced to great literature and became a voracious reader. Slowly, inside her, an idea formed. Cynthia dreamed of becoming a writer.

After college, Cynthia found a job in a local library. To her great delight, she was assigned to the children's room. And she fell in love—with children's books! "I can't tell you how I loved that room and all those books I never knew existed," Cynthia enthuses. "I carried bags full home at night just to read for pleasure."

Fearful of failure, Cynthia quietly set out to write a book of her own. It was to be a reflective book, drawing upon her Appalachian upbringing. She remembers, "One night I sat down and wrote *When I Was Young in the Mountains*. I sent it to a New York publisher and it sold."

Her work is widely praised and has garnered critical awards. But for Cynthia, writing itself has provided a far greater reward: "Writing has given me a sense of self-worth that I didn't have my whole childhood…The books have carried me through some troubled times and have made me feel that I am worthy of having a place on this earth."

Reading-Writing Connection

The people and pets in Cynthia Rylant's life often appear as characters in her stories. In fact, favorite characters in two of her books (*The Bookshop Dog* and *The Great Gracie Chase: Stop That Dog!*) are named for her dogs Martha Jane and Gracie Rose. Invite students to think about and make a list of important or interesting people and pets in their own lives. The pets don't have to be their own. Friends, relatives, or neighbors might have dogs, cats, or other pets that children have gotten to know. Now have students imagine these people and pets becoming characters in stories. What would these stories be about? Encourage students to use their ideas to write and illustrate stories of their own.

Photo of Cynthia Rylant, courtesy of Simon & Schuster. Profile of Cynthia Rylant excerpted from *The Big Book of Picture-Book Authors & Illustrators* by James Preller. Copyright © 2001 by James Preller. Used by permission of Scholastic Teaching Resources.

Activities to Use With Any Book

❧

When sharing books by Cynthia Rylant, consider the following ideas to strengthen reading skills, make writing connections, and more.

Cover Questions

Readers naturally look at a book's cover before they begin reading, so it's a good idea to teach children strategies for noticing clues in the title and cover illustration that can help them become active readers and make sense of the text.

1. When introducing a book, use the cover to model good reading behaviors. Read aloud the title and notice important words or features. For example, with *In November*, you may note that *November* is the name of a month. Ask: "What do we know about the month of November?" Invite children to share ideas.

2. Turn children's attention to the cover illustration. Ask: "What do you notice about the cover of this book?" For example, the cover of *In November* is bordered by brightly-colored fall leaves and a mouse peeks out from a corner.

3. Using information from the title and cover art, ask: "What do you think Cynthia Rylant is going to tell us about in this book?"

NOTE: For specific suggestions on introducing other titles, see the Before Reading section of each lesson.

This Reminds Me!

Many of Cynthia Rylant's books are based on experiences from her life, which create interesting opportunities for readers to make connections. Children may or may not have lived, for example, in rural West Virginia as the author did, but they can think about how characters or events remind them of something in their own lives in order to engage more actively with the text and better understand the story.

1. Take a moment during a read-aloud to make a text connection. For example, when reading *When I Was Young in the Mountains*, pause after reading about the narrator sitting on the porch swing as her grandfather sharpened pencils and her grandmother shelled beans. Think aloud about the way this scene reminds you of a memory from your own life—for example: *This reminds me of visits in the summer at my grandparents' home in the country. My brother*

(continued)

Tip

The following prompts can help children learn to make connections when they read.

- This reminds me of something that happened...
- This reminds me of something I saw...
- This makes me think of something else I read...
- This makes me think about that time when...

and I would sit on the front porch shelling peas we had just picked from the garden, while my grandfather told us stories and my grandmother started dinner. I enjoy thinking about those times, and I think this girl in the story treasures memories with her grandparents, too.

2. Let students practice making connections at the same point in the story by completing a sentence frame, such as "This part of the story reminds me of…"

Using the Reproducible Reader's Response Record

After sharing a story, invite students to complete the reproducible Reader's Response Record (page 14). As children begin to identify favorite books, characters, and authors, they'll discover more about themselves as readers and learn to select books that are just right for them.

Building Word Knowledge

In *Bringing Words to Life: Robust Vocabulary Instruction*, the authors "consider the best sources for new vocabulary to be trade books that teachers read aloud to children" (Beck, McKeown, & Kucan, 2002, p. 27). Cynthia Rylant's books are filled with evocative language that helps paint pictures of people, places, and special times, making them a rich resource for vocabulary development. The following activities can be used to create a vocabulary-rich environment based on words from Cynthia Rylant's books.

Following Up on Unfamiliar Words: While reading, if you encounter a word that may be unfamiliar to children, give a quick explanation and continue. For example, when reading *Miss Maggie*, pause to briefly explain the meaning of *avoid*—to keep away from or not do—then continue the story. After reading, you might revisit the text to show how readers use context clues, pictures, and other strategies to figure out the meaning of unknown words. In the case of *avoid*, the context from the story will likely help children make sense of the word: Nat is careful to "avoid the tricky board" when he walks across Miss Maggie's porch to knock on the door. Follow up by using the word in different situations that relate to children: "To avoid getting paint on the table, let's put newspaper down first." "To avoid getting sick, be sure to wash your hands."

Fun With Words: Encourage children to have fun with language from the stories (and other words) by creating an environment that invites word play. As you share stories and introduce new vocabulary, copy the words on index cards. Periodically, review these words with children. Then invite a child to choose a card at random, read the word silently, and draw a picture (or perform an action) that will help others guess the word.

Word Wall Charts: As you read, look for words that might be used to create a wall chart. Words grouped by a common theme provide children with a framework for making connections to other new, but related, words. For example, sensory words that relate to the month of November (inspired by vocabulary from *In November*) might make an inviting wall chart. Use the charts as a meaningful way to pass a few extra minutes between activities. You might define a word and have students hunt for the word. Or you could time children to see how fast they can read the words. Record the time and then have the class repeat the activity on another day to try to beat that time.

☀ **Everyday Words:** Use words from read-alouds in everyday situations. Frequent encounters with a word, in contexts other than the book, are necessary if children are to really learn the word (Beck, et al, 2002). For instance, if a parent volunteer helps out every week, you might remark to the class, "We're so lucky that Mrs. Wong *faithfully* comes to our classroom every Wednesday." (This word appears in *The Old Woman Who Named Things.*) You could also say that Mrs. Wong is a *devoted* volunteer! (This word appears in *The Bookshop Dog.*)

After-Reading Skill Builders

Spark discussion and strengthen comprehension skills with these activities.

☀ **If the Title Fits...:** After reading a book, revisit the title. Encourage students to discuss whether the title fits the story. What other titles might Cynthia Rylant have considered? Take a vote: Would students have chosen the same title? Why or why not?

☀ **What Really Happened?:** After reading, summarize or retell the story together, being sure to cover the beginning, middle, and end. Along the way, encourage children to compare any predictions they may have made about the story with what actually happened. What were they right about? Did anything surprise them? Let children know that it's okay to revise predictions as they read. That means they are paying attention to the details and thinking about what is happening.

☀ **Character Clues:** Review characters in the story and ask children to choose one to get to know better. Ask: "What did the author tell you about this character? What clues in the story and illustrations helped you learn about this character? How do you think the author wants you to feel about this character? How do you know?"

☀ **Sentence Strip Retellings:** Retelling a story helps children learn to identify the main ideas and most important details. As children retell a story, record their sentences on chart paper. Later, copy the sentences on sentence strips, mix up the sentence strips, and place them in a pocket chart. Where possible, draw a simple picture on each sentence strip to provide support for the text. Encourage children to put the sentences in order to retell the story. (Number the back of the sentence strips for self-checking purposes.)

Fluency Practice

From stories that feature much-loved pets to those about family and friends, Rylant's books offer many reasons to read with feeling. In addition to text features that provide clues to expression, you'll find many opportunities to demonstrate how to use phrasing, pacing, and inflection to make sense of the text as well as to provide students with fluency practice.

☼ **Reading With Expression:** To provide practice with inflection and tone, preview a story for examples of text that invite exaggerated expression. For instance, in *Mr. Putter & Tabby Pick the Pears*, the word *ZING!!!!!* (in all uppercase letters followed by five exclamation marks) is a great example of how text features and punctuation affect meaning. In many of Rylant's books, you'll find text that appears in uppercase lettering, italicized, and punctuated with exclamation marks (such as *"THERE'S GRACIE!"* from *The Great Gracie Chase: Stop That Dog!*).

☼ **"Scat!":** Use dialogue to show how changes in inflection and pitch make characters come alive. Point out that quotation marks signal when characters are speaking, and punctuation helps readers know where to pause or end a phrase. Let children read the parts of different characters to practice intonation, phrasing, and expression.

☼ **Constructing Meaning, With Commas:**

> "Four of us once draped a very long snake, dead of course,
> across our necks for a photograph."
> (from *When I Was Young in the Mountains*)

Cynthia Rylant's writing paints vivid pictures for readers, and attention to punctuation will help them get the full effect of the author's intentions. Point out how commas help readers with phrasing. Let children try reading aloud some of these sentences with, and without, pausing in the appropriate places.

All About the Illustrators

As readers enjoy Cynthia Rylant books, take time to make connections to the illustrators, who include Kathryn Brown, Stephen Gammell, Diane Goode, Jill Kastner, Mark Siegel, Suçie Stevenson, Mary Szilagyi, and Mark Teague.

1. Let children pair up and choose an illustrator of one of Cynthia Rylant's books to research.

2. Visit the library and guide children in locating books illustrated by that person. Encourage them to choose a couple of selections to share with the class. (Check in advance to make sure books are available for the illustrators students have selected. See note, left, for a closer look at one illustrator.)

Get to Know Diane Goode

Diane Goode illustrated the Caldecott Honor book *When I Was Young in the Mountains*. A sampling of the more than 40 picture books she's illustrated (and sometimes written) follows.

- *My Mom Is Trying to Ruin My Life* by Kate Feiffer (Simon & Schuster, 2008)

- *President Pennybaker* by Kate Feiffer (Simon & Schuster, 2008)

- *Alligator Boy* by Cynthia Rylant (Harcourt, 2007)

- *Thanksgiving Is Here!* by Diane Goode (HarperCollins, 2005)

- *Mind Your Manners!* by Diane Goode (Farrar, Straus & Giroux, 2005)

- *Tiger Trouble!* by Diane Goode (Scholastic, 2001)

Tips for Teaching With Chapter Books

"When can I read a big-kid book?" The first chapter book is a highly anticipated milestone of childhood. With their distinct features, including a table of contents, chapter books signal an exciting transition for children. These books stretch a young child's growing literacy skills, building both reading stamina and confidence in tackling more challenging text. Children are naturally motivated to read to the end of a chapter, which helps them set satisfying goals for reading. The incentive to continue reading is strong: From one chapter to the next, characters become like friends, keeping readers motivated to read on and discover what happens next. Anticipation of the next book in a series helps to heighten children's interest and enthusiasm for reading.

Pages 59–76 feature lessons for teaching with three early chapter-book series: Poppleton, Mr. Putter & Tabby, and Henry and Mudge. Following are strategies and activities to provide further support for teaching reading with the books in these series.

Exploring Story Elements

As children read books in a series, the characters, settings, and plot devices become familiar. This familiarity provides a boost to reading skills, as children can use what they know to more independently make predictions, connect to the text, and draw conclusions. Create a chart to compare story elements as children read books in a series. Use the chart to help children understand the ways in which these components work together. (See sample, right.)

- **Who?:** Analyze the characters in each story: Which characters appear in each book? Each chapter? Which characters come and go? How are the characters alike? How are they different? What details do readers discover in each book that help them get to know the characters better?

(continued)

Tip

For children who are transitioning to chapter books, ease into the increased demands of reading by taking turns. You might invite the child to read the dialogue for one character, while you read the remaining text. More able readers might like to reverse those roles. Two children can pair up in the same way for "buddy" reading. This allows children to experience success with chapter books, even if they are not ready to tackle an entire book on their own.

Story Elements

	Poppleton		
Who?	Poppleton (a pig) Cherry Sue (a llama) Fillmore (a goat)		
Where?	A small town: ◆ Poppleton's house ◆ Cherry Sue's house ◆ the library ◆ Fillmore's house		
What?	◆ Poppleton moves from the city to a small town, meets new neighbor. ◆ He spends the day at the library. ◆ He helps a sick friend and gets sick, too.		

Bookmark Pattern

Copy the pattern on page 15 and let children make bookmarks they can use to monitor their own reading. Have them color and cut out the pattern, fold at the center, then glue the backs together. Keep extra copies on hand so that children can make new bookmarks as needed.

Where?: With each book in a series, readers get better acquainted with where the stories take place. In the process, they also discover interesting details about the characters. For example, readers learn a lot about the personable Poppleton as he spends time at home and when he's out and about in his town. Pictures in his house, for example, tell readers that he enjoys the shore and sailing (*Poppleton and Friends*).

What?: What comparisons can be made between story events in each book? What problems do characters face? What do they do to solve these problems? What does this tell readers about a character? Poppleton, for example, has a problem with an overly attentive neighbor but is too polite to say anything. The surprising solution leads to their lasting friendship—and reveals much about these key characters.

Stories on Stage

With three to five chapters per book, the Poppleton, Mr. Putter & Tabby, and Henry and Mudge series are perfectly suited for performing mini-plays.

1. Have children work in small groups to act out each chapter in a book, assigning parts for a narrator and each character. Guide children in learning how they can create dialogue for characters based on the text.

2. Children can create simple paper-bag costumes to represent their characters. (Later, store these at the dramatic play center so that children can continue to act out scenes from the stories.)

   - For each character, cut an opening in the bottom of a paper grocery bag large enough for children to fit their heads through. Then cut out armholes in the sides of the bag.
   - Use colored markers to draw a picture of the character on the front.

3. As children practice their performances, take time to reinforce speaking and listening skills. To make a writing connection, have children create posters or programs for their performances.

Skill-Building Lists

List-making is a rewarding and fun writing activity in which every child can participate and experience success. These activities strengthen comprehension skills as children analyze details in the text and illustrations to explore story elements across a series.

- **Favorites:** Children enjoy sharing their favorites—colors, foods, games, and so on. It's fun to think about a character's favorites, too. Encourage children to use clues in the story to learn more about the characters in this way. Start a list of favorites with the first book in a series, and add to it as children read other titles. As the list grows, encourage children to recognize just how much they're continuing to learn about the character.

Mr. Putter's Favorites

Favorite Animal	Favorite Person	Favorite Things	Favorite Foods	Favorite Times of Year
Tabby, his cat	Mrs. Teaberry	◆ free samples ◆ rain ◆ opera ◆ model airplanes	◆ tea ◆ apple pie ◆ apple turnovers ◆ apple cider ◆ stuffed tomatoes ◆ pear jelly	◆ fall ◆ winter (Christmastime; he likes to give presents)

- **Where and When?:** What do the text and illustrations tell about the setting of a story? Have children generate a list of details that describe where the story takes place. Ask questions to elicit basic information: "Could this place be real? What does it remind you of? What do you know about places like this? Could this story happen now or would it have happened long ago?" Remind children to look for clues in the text and pictures. For example, the text tells readers that Poppleton moved to a small town. And when he spends the day at the beach, they also learn that the town is near a body of water. To determine when the series takes place, encourage children to examine the text and pictures for clues, such as a television and telephone.

- **Check the Pockets:** What might children find if they emptied their pockets: A small toy, a shiny stone, or a half-eaten granola bar? A story might not tell readers what's in a character's pockets, but it's fun to imagine. In the process, readers develop a deeper understanding of characterization and plot. Have children make a list of things that a character might have in his or her pockets. For each item, ask them to provide supporting evidence from the story. For example, Henry (in the Henry and Mudge series) might well have a few dog biscuits in his pockets. Why? His best friend, Mudge, is a dog! (At various times, he also has a flower petal, flashlight, magnifying glass, and crackers in his pockets, all of which are related to the plot in some way.) Based on what they know about Henry, readers might predict that he'd have a few toys and cookies in his pockets, too.

Name _____ Date _____

Reader's Response Record

Book Title: _____

Author: _____ **Illustrator:** _____

1 How many stars do you give this book?
(1 = did not like; 5 = liked a lot)
Color the stars to show how many.

2 Tell something about the beginning, middle, and end of the story.

Beginning: _____

_____

Middle: _____

_____

End: _____

_____

3 What three words best describe this book?

1. _____ 2. _____ 3. _____

4 Would you like to read another story like this? Why or why not?

_____

_____

5 What is something the author does in this book that you would like to try in your own

writing? _____

_____

Teaching Reading With Cynthia Rylant Books © 2009 by Joan Novelli, Scholastic Teaching Resources

Readers Think About Words

Book Title: _____

_____

Words I Figured Out

1 _____

2 _____

3 _____

Words I Need Help With

1 _____

2 _____

3 _____

Name: _____

Book Title: _____

_____

Readers Ask Questions

☐ What do I think the story is about?

☐ What has happened so far?

☐ How do the pictures help me understand?

☐ What does this remind me of?

☐ What do I think will happen next?

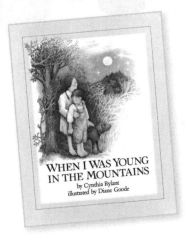

When I Was Young in the Mountains

(DUTTON, 1982)

From hot corn bread, fried okra, and the smell of sweet milk to dark, muddy swimming holes alive with snakes, the images in this story bring to life a time and place filled with treasured memories.

Before Reading

Give students a glimpse of the place the author has written about by taking a picture walk through the book, beginning with the cover. Read the title first, and have students identify key words. Ask: "What do these words tell you about this story? What kind of story do you think this will be? What does the picture on the cover tell you about this story?" Continue letting students make predictions about the story as you preview the pages.

During Reading

While the events in this story occurred in a time and place that may be unfamiliar to children, the pictures provide strong support for understanding the text. As you read, encourage students to examine the pictures for details that help them learn more about where and when this story took place. (See Where and When?, page 17, for a follow-up activity.)

After Reading

Focus questions after reading on the sensory-rich memories that the author shares with readers. Discuss any questions children have to enhance their understanding. Here are a few questions you might ask:

✺ What is different about this book from other books we've read? (Guide students to notice that there is not a "problem and a solution" as in many books. Instead, this is a collection of memories.)

- What kinds of memories did the author write about?

- Why do you think Grandfather is covered with black dust? (Discuss coal mining, which may be unfamiliar to some students.)

- What do you think made mealtime a special memory? Do you have some special mealtime memories?

- Does it seem as though the girl was scared by the dark, muddy water, or the snake? How do you know? What are some things that could have been scary for you but weren't?

- What could a johnny-house be? What would it be like to go to the johnny-house at night?

- Why do you think the characters had to pump water from a well? What do you think it was like to take a bath this way? How is this the same or different from the way we live?

- If you were the narrator of this story, what would be your favorite memory of all?

Where and When?

The time and place of this story is lovingly portrayed through poetic text and illustrations that paint a picture of contentment. Further explore the story's setting with an activity that reinforces map-reading skills.

1. After sharing the story, invite children to revisit illustrations and point out details that tell them where and when the story takes place. Ask: "What mountains do you think the author is writing about?"

2. Remind students that the author grew up in West Virginia. (See Meet Cynthia Rylant, page 6.) Help students first locate West Virginia on a map, and then identify mountains.

3. Invite students to trace on the map with their fingers or a pointer the mountains in West Virginia. They can also follow the Appalachians from here through other parts of the Eastern United States (14 states in all).

4. Make a connection to students' own writing. Ask: "If you were going to write a book about your early memories, where would it take place? What are some characteristics of this place?"

Walked, Jumped, Whistled

As a warm-up to writing their own stories about memories, plan a mini-lesson on verbs—in this case, the author's use of past tense verbs in *When I Was Young in the Mountains*.

1. Invite students to share what they know about verbs. Review that a verb is a word that shows action or a state of being.

(continued)

2. Let students act out a few verbs from the story, such as *walk*, *jump*, and *whistle*. Then have them sit down and tell you what they did. ("We walked." "We jumped." "We whistled.") Write the words on chart paper, identify the past tense verbs, and explain that these words tell what has already happened.

3. Reread passages in the book and invite children to give you a sign (such as raising their hands) when they hear a word that names an action that has already taken place. Ask: "Why do you think the author used past tense verbs in this story?" Guide students to understand that it's a way of letting readers know that she is writing about memories—things that happened in the past.

Mini-Memoirs

Use *When I Was Young in the Mountains* as a model for children's own keepsake picture-book memoirs.

1. In preparation for this writing activity, create a blank book for each child. You can simply staple plain paper together, or for a sturdier book, follow these steps.

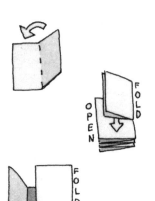

- For each interior page, fold a sheet of white paper in half (fold each sheet separately). Stack the folded papers with the folds facing right.

- To make the cover, fold a new sheet of paper (tagboard or construction paper) in half. Place the fold to the left.

- Place the interior pages inside the cover (folds facing right) and staple along the left side to bind. Each folded sheet creates a page that has a little more heft than a single layer of paper.

2. Reread the beginning of the story. Revisit pages on which the text "When I was young in the mountains…" is repeated.

3. Give each child a copy of the Mini-Memoirs Planner (page 20). Have students complete the heading on the right with the name of a place. Using the prompts on the left, have them complete the planner to tell about favorite memories.

4. Have children use their planner as a reference to complete their books. They can copy their sentences on the left-facing pages and illustrate them on the right-facing pages. Remind them to use past-tense verbs just as the author did to tell about their memories.

5. Revisit the cover of *When I Was Young in the Mountains* and invite children to explain how the illustration here matches the story. Have children think about what's important in their own stories before they create a cover for their books.

Vocabulary Builder: Names for Places

"Place" is an important element in many of Cynthia Rylant's stories, and that is especially true with *When I Was Young in the Mountains*. To develop awareness of specific nouns and of settings, create a wall chart for words that name places. Add to the chart as children read more books by the author.

1. After reading, ask students to recall places the author mentioned—for example:

coal mine	mountains
cow pasture	schoolhouse
johnny-house	swimming hole

2. Record names for places in the story on chart paper. Incorporate mini-lessons on proper nouns and capitalization as applicable.

3. Display the chart and use it to spark a discussion about the importance of specific words in writing. For example, ask: "Why do you think the author used *cow pasture* instead of *field*? *Johnny-house* instead of *bathroom*?" Encourage students to recognize that specific language can make a story more interesting and paint vivid pictures in a reader's mind.

4. Encourage children to use the wall chart as inspiration for settings in their own stories and as a reminder to capitalize proper nouns.

Book Links

Share these books to spend more time getting to know the place that inspired *When I Was Young in the Mountains*.

- *Appalachia: Voices of Sleeping Birds* by Cynthia Rylant (Sandpiper, 1998): This lovely pairing of text and art captures life in this region, where both the author and illustrator, Barry Moser, grew up.

- *In Coal Country* by Judith Hendershot (Dragonfly, 1992): This *New York Times* Notable Book of the Year gives readers a glimpse of growing up in coal country.

- *My Great-Aunt Arizona* by Gloria Houston (HarperCollins, 1997): Arizona "was born in a log cabin her papa built…in the Blue Ridge Mountains." She teaches in the same schoolhouse where she went to school as a young girl, and her students learn about far-away places she longed to visit herself.

Author: Cynthia Rylant

Names for Places

When I Was Young in the Mountains:

coal mine

cow pasture

johnny-house

mountains

Name _____   Date _____

Mini-Memoirs Planner

Types of Memories	When I Was Young in _____
A special person I knew	
A special place I went	
Special foods I ate	
Something fun I did	
Sounds I heard	
A way that I helped	
Something I learned	
Other	

Teaching Reading With Cynthia Rylant Books © 2009 by Joan Novelli, Scholastic Teaching Resources

Miss Maggie

(DUTTON, 1983)

"**M**aggie Ziegler lived in a rotting log house on the edge of Crawford's pasture." Here, rumor has it, a snake hangs in the rafters to keep the mice out of the cupboards. Miss Maggie's neighbor, Nat, hopes to catch a glimpse of the snake, but fear keeps him from going past the front porch. Then one day, concern for his neighbor prevails, and an unlikely friendship has its beginnings.

Before Reading

Use the book's simple, straightforward title to introduce the topic of characterization. Share the cover, read the title aloud, and ask: "How does the title help you predict what the author wants to tell you about in this story?" Briefly discuss what students can learn about the main character from the cover illustration (such as how old she is, where she lives, what her life might be like, even how she may feel).

During Reading

Encourage children to confirm their predictions about Miss Maggie as you read. In addition to details provided in the illustrations, guide students to notice what the descriptions, action, and dialogue tell them about Miss Maggie. For example, early in the story, children learn about the vegetable garden that Miss Maggie faithfully tends, despite the fact that not much grows "what with the cows, dogs, and boys passing through." From this they might gather that things don't bother her too much—she seems even-tempered. Look for other opportunities throughout the book to add to children's understanding of this lovingly portrayed character.

After Reading

Continue to explore the story's main characters, using the following questions as a guide to help children understand how thinking about a character's traits can help them understand a story.

☀ What do we know about Miss Maggie so far? (Have children confirm or revise their earlier predictions about this character, and point out clues in the text and pictures that helped them learn more about her.)

(continued)

✧ What do we know about Nat? (Nat is a child, so encourage children to put themselves in his place to better understand how he thinks and feels.) Children might share that Nat is curious (he peeks in the windows hoping to see the snake), a little shy (he runs away when Miss Maggie invites him in), embarrassed (he was afraid people in town would think they were related), caring (he worries when he doesn't see her chimney puffing), brave (he was scared to go in the house but he did because he thought she might need help), and so on.

Dialogue Detectives

Explain to children that good readers get to know the personalities of characters through dialogue. They wonder, "What does this person sound like? What does that tell me?" Information in the text gives readers clues. Challenge students to be detectives with the text in *Miss Maggie*, looking for evidence of how the characters sound when they speak.

1. Choose an example of dialogue from the story, such as the scene in which Nat finds Miss Maggie huddled in the corner. Reread the section of the story that contains that dialogue.

2. Ask: "How do you think Nat sounds when he calls out to Miss Maggie?" Have students look for clues in the text:

   • The story says Nat tried to call out but his throat froze. (Discuss what this means.) When he does speak, he might sound a little scared, but also concerned.

   • The story says Nat takes Miss Maggie's hand. This tells readers he is kind and helpful. When he says "C'mon…My grandad will know what to do," his voice might sound reassuring.

3. Examine the text for clues that tell readers how Miss Maggie might sound.

   • The text says Miss Maggie is huddled next to the empty fireplace. This tells readers that she must be cold and might be shivering.

   • Miss Maggie doesn't move when Nat calls to her; she's probably weak. When she speaks, her voice might be quiet and shaky.

4. Invite pairs of volunteers to take turns reading aloud the dialogue between Nat and Miss Maggie, using what they now know to give "voice" to the characters.

Five-Senses Scavenger Hunt

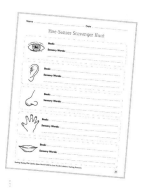

In *What a Writer Needs* (Heinemann, 1993), Ralph Fletcher calls them a writer's "most important tools." They're the five senses—and with them, your students can both read for the details that bring characters to life and use them in their own writing to create believable characters. To help students learn more about how writers use the five senses, send them on a scavenger hunt.

1. Read aloud a passage from *Miss Maggie*. Choose any passage with strong sensory images. Here's an example:

   > Nat would see Miss Maggie rising up from the soil, her brown, wrinkled face partly hidden by a faded blue bonnet, and he'd watch while she shuffled back to the house with an apron filled with a few vegetables that had survived.

2. Have students identify words from the story that appeal to their senses—words that let them see, hear, taste, smell, and feel what's happening. In the case of the example above, readers can imagine the smell of the soil. They can picture Miss Maggie's lined face under the bonnet, and they can both see and hear her as she shuffles away—all images that help paint a picture of a character that readers will come to care about.

3. Now have students pair up to search books they're reading for examples of sensory details. Have students record their findings on the Five-Senses Scavenger Hunt record sheet (page 25). When finished, bring students together to share and discuss their examples.

Miss Maggie: Part 2

Revisit the cover of *Miss Maggie* and the last scene showing Miss Maggie and Nat. Invite children to wonder what a sequel to *Miss Maggie* would be like. Then invite them to create the cover for such a book, including a title and picture that help tell what's next for these endearing characters.

1. Discuss children's ideas for a sequel to *Miss Maggie*. Encourage them to support their ideas with evidence from the actual book. Ask: "What have you learned about Miss Maggie and Nat that helps you think about ideas for another book about these characters? How would this new book be different from the first one? What would be the same?"

2. Have children sketch their ideas and brainstorm titles before creating their final covers.

3. Invite children to share and discuss their work. If time allows, consider a collaborative writing activity to create the sequel.

Vocabulary Builder: Vivid Verbs

Miss Maggie isn't just sitting in the corner—she "huddled" and "clutched a bundle" in her hands. This story is full of vivid verbs that invite an active approach to building vocabulary.

1. Select verbs from the story to teach, especially those that children can easily act out—for example, *peered, shuffled, wriggled, huddled,* and *clutched*.

2. Use the following procedure as a guide to teach these words.

   - Say the word. Remind students how it is used in the story and what it means in that context.

   - Have students say the word with you.

   - Invite students to act out the word. They might also describe situations in which they use the word (for example, they might *peer* through a door or *shuffle* down the hall).

3. Throughout the day, encourage children to have fun demonstrating the words they have learned. For example, you might invite them to *peer* out the window to look at a bird or suggest that they *clutch* their lunch bags as they walk to the cafeteria.

Book Links

Introduce students to more memorable characters with these books, each a Caldecott winner.

- *Madeline* by Ludwig Bemelmans (Viking, 1967): The cheerful and brave young heroine in this classic has a personality that sparkles— whether she's making mischief or taking a trip to the hospital.

- *Mirette on the Highwire* by Emily Arnold McCully (Putnam, 1992): Young Mirette discovers a guest at her mother's boarding house "crossing the courtyard on air" and begs him to teach her how to do it, too. Unknown to Mirette, her teacher is the Great Bellini, whose fear has put a halt to his high-wire act. Though he is the teacher, it is Mirette who gives him courage, and together they "cross the sky."

- *Song and Dance Man* by Karen Ackerman (Knopf, 1988): In this enchanting story, three children and their grandpa go up to the attic, where he grabs his hat and cane and puts on a song and dance show from his vaudeville days. Full of life, this book is a wonderful example of how text and illustrations bring characters to life.

Name _____ Date _____

Five-Senses Scavenger Hunt

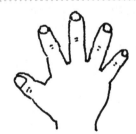

Book: _____

Sensory Words: _____

_____

Book: _____

Sensory Words: _____

_____

Book: _____

Sensory Words: _____

_____

Book: _____

Sensory Words: _____

_____

Book: _____

Sensory Words: _____

_____

The Relatives Came

(BRADBURY PRESS, 1985)

This lively account of an annual family get-together is full of affection and the carefree feeling that comes with summer vacation. Readers can feel the anticipation as the relatives load up the station wagon in the dark and drive "all day and into the night" and "all those miles" until they arrive and are met with lots of hugging. The weeks that follow are full of laughing, crying, cooking, eating, sleeping, talking, helping, and more hugging. Then, dreams about next summer's visit and more memories to be made fill the long trip home. The joyful mood is well-matched by Stephen Gammell's Caldecott Honor-winning illustrations.

Before Reading

The cover of *The Relatives Came* is full of hints of what's to come. Ask questions to guide children in using information in both the illustration and title to make predictions.

- Direct attention to the illustration. Ask: "What's happening here? Who do you think these people are? Where do you think they are going? What do you think is on top of the car? Do you think these people are taking a long or short trip? How can you tell?"

- Read aloud the title. Ask: "What words in the title tell you about the people and what they might be doing?" Explain that story titles often include words that help readers predict what a story is about.

Encourage children to listen and look for clues as you read the story to confirm (or revise) their predictions.

During Reading

As you read, model different types of connections readers can make—from the relatives' long journey to their arrival and the fun-filled weeks that follow. You might, for example, recall a trip you've taken: "This reminds me of the trip I take with my kids every summer to visit my mother. Just like the family in this book, we leave before it is light out. In fact, it's so early in the morning, Ann and William are still in their pajamas! And they go right back to sleep as soon as they get settled in the car." (See Tip, page 7, for a list of prompts to help children make text connections.)

Tip

Good news for students eager for more books illustrated by Stephen Gammell! There are dozens, including these:

- *I Know an Old Teacher* by Anne Bowen (Carolrhoda, 2008)
- *My Friend, the Starfinder* by George Ella Lyon (Simon and Schuster, 2008)
- *The Secret Science Project That Almost Ate the School* by Judy Sierra (Simon & Schuster, 2006)
- *Once Upon Macdonald's Farm* by Stephen Gammell (Simon & Schuster, 2000)

Whether they're sharing a big supper, fixing a fence, or plucking a banjo, the relatives in this story stay busy. As you revisit pages in the book, ask questions to focus attention on details in the text and illustrations that help readers engage with the characters.

- What do you think the relatives are thinking as they begin their trip? How do you know?

- Have you ever had a visit like this one? What was that like? How do these pictures remind you of your visit?

- How do you think the relatives feel when they first see each other? What are some clues?

- What do you think it means when the author writes, "It was different, going to sleep with all that new breathing in the house"? (Encourage children to think about their own experiences with sleepovers.)

- What do you think the relatives are thinking as they are driving away? How do you know?

- If these were your relatives, what would you like best about visiting them?

Morning Message Character Count

When it comes to characters, this story might take the record. There are relatives of all ages, and with all the activity going on, it's a challenge to keep track of them. This morning message activity warms up children's problem-solving skills while engaging them in revisiting the book for new details.

1. The day after sharing *The Relatives Came*, pose a problem in the morning message: "How many relatives are there in all? Think of a way we could find the answer." Write the problem in the Morning Message. Then provide a sticky note for each child to share their solution. (See Tip, right.)

2. Later in the day, for example at the Morning Meeting, invite children to share their responses and explain their problem-solving strategies.

3. Then, as a class, put your problem-solving skills together to figure out how many relatives there are. For example, you might set up a chart to collect data by approximate age: How many babies? Little kids? Big kids? Grown-ups?

4. As an extension, invite children to suggest names for the characters and explain why the names fit. (They might find it interesting that the characters in this book don't have names.) This will strengthen students' own writing skills, as they learn to give careful consideration to the characters they develop in their stories.

Tip

To give all children a chance to respond to the Morning Message question, write each child's name on a large sticky note, and place below the message. When children come to school in the morning, they (1) read the message, (2) find their sticky note, (3) take it back to their table, (4) write a response on the back, and (5) replace their sticky note on the morning message. This approach solves the problem of too many children at the morning message easel at one time, and allows for the time and space children need to write a thoughtful response.

(from *Quick Tips: Morning Message* by Anne Adams, Diane Farnham, Carol McQuillen, and Donna Peabody; Scholastic, 2003).

Hugging Time

"Talk about hugging!" There's also crying, laughing, more hugging, breathing, eating, and hugging some more, until it's time for the relatives to go home, which leads to…*missing*. By learning to identify the suffix in a word, children can more easily identify the base word and figure out the meaning. The suffix *-ing* appears frequently in *The Relatives Came*, and is among the 20 most frequent suffixes (Blevins, 2006), making it a good choice for a word analysis mini-lesson that also provides a movement break.

1. Reread the book and have students listen for words that end with the suffix *-ing*. (See list, left.)

2. List the words on chart paper and read them together. Ask: "What do you notice about these words?" Guide children to recognize that the words all end in *-ing*.

3. Briefly introduce the term *suffix* and explain that adding a suffix like *-ing* changes the form of a word—for example, from *laugh* to *laughing*. Together, identify the base word for each word on the list and write these words separately on the chart (next to the corresponding words). Point out cases in which adding *-ing* changes the spelling of the base word, as is the case, for example, with *shining* (deleting the silent *e*) and *hugging* (doubling the final consonant).

4. Write each word on a large index card. Show children the cards, one at a time. Have them read the word together and act it out.

Story Words That End in *-ing*

waiting	shining
hugging	breathing
pulling	eating
crying	missing
laughing	

Shoe Box Storytelling

Retelling a story helps readers identify important ideas and details, provides opportunities for oral language development, and serves as an informal assessment of how well they understand a story. This activity gives children practice in retelling a story with a shoe box full of props.

1. Cover a shoe box with colorful paper. Write the title of the story on an index card and tape or glue it to the lid.

2. Stock the shoe box with small objects that represent events

Sample Storytelling Props

- toy car (station wagon, if possible)
- clean, empty snack bags
- toy mountain (such as from a "mountain" train set)
- small packet of tissues (to represent the relatives' arrival)
- spoon (to represent their big suppers)
- small teddy bear (to represent bed time)
- toy hoe or shovel (to represent gardening)
- toy hammer (to represent fixing things)
- toy camera (to represent all the things they do together)
- bunch of plastic purple grapes (to represent the return home)

in the story. (See suggested props, page 28.) You can also use the picture cards provided on page 30. (See Tip, right.)

3. Model how to use the objects in the shoe box to retell the story, thinking about what happened first, next, and so on to retell events in order.

4. Place the shoe box at a center and let children visit independently or in pairs to practice retelling the story.

Vocabulary Builder: "Family" Connections

The theme of "Family" is a natural for broadening children's vocabularies, since it connects to their own lives and experiences. Create a colorful wall chart to develop vocabulary for this theme, starting with the word *relatives*.

1. Discuss with children what they know about the word *relatives*. Share a definition (people who are connected to each other by family), and invite children to use the word in a sentence to tell about relatives they know (from their own families or friends' families, other books, and so on).

2. Write the word *relatives* on chart paper. Draw a picture of a multigenerational family next to the word (or use one cut from a magazine or old workbook).

3. Brainstorm with children words that name relatives. Revisit pictures in the book for ideas, such as *cousin*, *grandma*, *grandpa*, *aunt*, and *uncle*. Add the words to the chart and invite children to illustrate them.

4. Play games to reinforce the meanings of the words. For example, say, "If I am your aunt, who are you to me?" (Answer: *your niece or nephew*)

Book Links

Share more stories about memorable storybook relatives.

☼ *Abuela* by Arthur Dorros (Dutton, 1991): In this exuberant story, a young girl imagines flying over Manhattan with her Abuela (grandmother), who shares memories sparked by the sights.

☼ *Nana Upstairs & Nana Downstairs* by Tomie dePaola (Putnam, 1997): Originally published in 1973, this revised edition has new, full-color illustrations but tells the same poignant story of a young boy who visits his nanas (grandmother and great-grandmother) every Sunday.

☼ *When Lightning Strikes in a Jar* by Patricia Polacco (Philomel, 2002): At this year's family reunion, Gramma promises to teach the kids how to catch "lightning" in a jar. Based on the author's own childhood experiences, the story invites readers in for a get-together filled with favorite foods, games, and lots of family stories.

Tip

If using the picture cards (page 30) to stock the shoe box, try this simple idea to turn each card into an "object" that's easier for small hands to hold: Gather ten clean, dry small juice boxes and cover each with colorful paper. Color and cut apart the picture cards, and glue each to a box. Plain picture cards are now fun storytelling props!

Tip

Research supports a theme-based approach to teaching vocabulary. "Word consciousness develops even more deeply when vocabulary words are tied to a common theme." (Block and Mangieri, 2004) By learning words associated with the theme "Families," children will develop a framework for understanding new vocabulary that relates to this group of words.

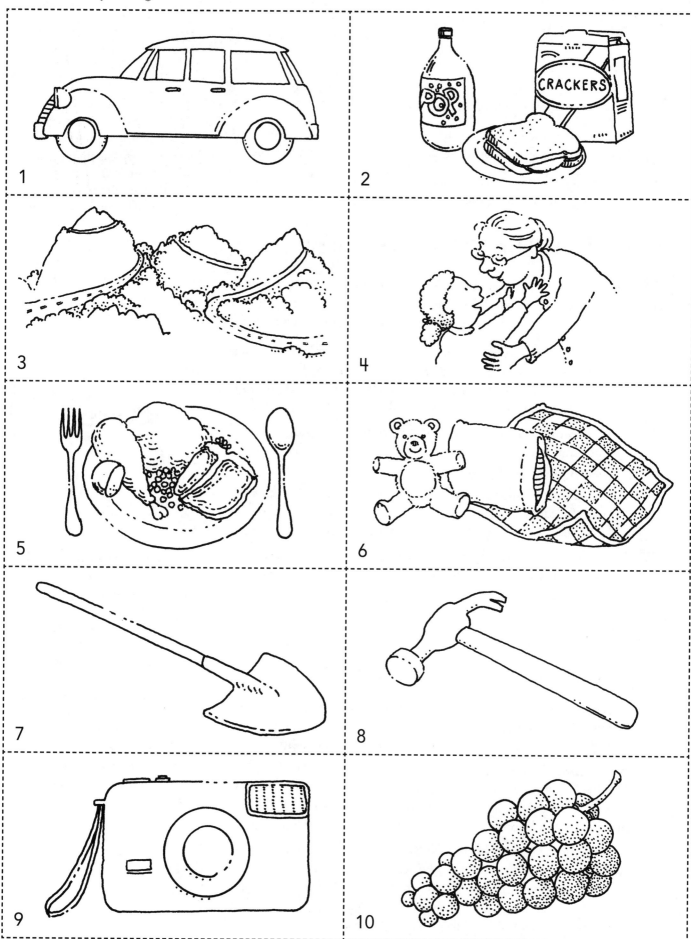

1

2

3

4

5

6

7

8

9

10

Night in the Country

(BRADBURY PRESS, 1986)

NIGHT IN THE COUNTRY
story by CYNTHIA RYLANT
pictures by MARY SZILAGYI

"There is no night so dark, so black as night in the country." From the sounds of night birds swooping and frogs singing to a dog's chain clinking and a screen door creaking, lyrical text and lush pictures envelop readers in a soothing portrait of nighttime.

Before Reading

Shadowy grass, a glowing sky, a small dog scooting inside. . . Give children time to savor the cover illustration, then invite them to close their eyes and make pictures in their minds as you read aloud just the first page. Next, provide paper and colored pencils (or crayons). Reread the text and, as a way of predicting, have children draw the "nighttime things" they imagine the author *writes* about. Then read the story in its entirety and let children just listen and enjoy.

During Reading

Read the story through before returning to revisit some of the sights and sounds of night in the country. Let children compare the pictures they drew in the Before Reading activity to those in the story. Do they see some of the same creatures? What sounds did they expect to hear? What sounds are new? It's interesting to note the perspective in different illustrations: Where is the river? The farmhouse? The tractor? The fence? Children will have fun discovering the viewpoint in each scene.

After Reading

Discussion "Starters"

Whether children live in the country, the city, or someplace in between, they'll be captivated by this book. The dark, shadowy pictures give the story elements of a mystery, and the soothing text reads almost like a lullaby. Exploring favorite parts of a book helps children become active readers. Use the questions here to help children reflect on what they like best about the story and to learn more about themselves as readers.

- How is this story like others we've read? How is it different? (Guide children to see that, unlike many stories, this one is not about a problem and solution.)

- Share what you especially like about the story, such as a particular passage or picture, and tell why. Then ask: "What is your favorite part of this story? Why?" Encourage students to explain their choices.

Country in the Classroom

With frogs singing "*reek reek reek reek*" and apples falling off trees with a "*Pump!*", this story brings nighttime to life with sensory-rich language. Have fun adding sound effects to a rereading to create "nighttime in the country" right in your classroom!

1. As you reread the story, have children listen carefully for nighttime sounds—either in the "sound words" the author uses or through sounds the text helps them imagine.

2. Follow up by listing the sounds on chart paper:

   - owls swooping
   - frogs singing ("*reek reek reek reek*")
   - dog's chain clinking
   - screen door creaking
   - apples falling ("*Pump!*")
   - rabbits patter
   - groans, thumps, squeaks
   - animals in the barn nuzzling, rolling over
   - one bird telling everyone "night in the country is nearly over"

3. Involve children in planning a read-aloud with sound effects. For example, students can form small groups to make each sound as you read aloud the text. Be sure to discuss how the sound effects change at the end of the story: As one bird announces the approach of day, the owls go to sleep, the frogs grow quiet, and the rabbits run away.

4. Practice reading the story with sound effects a few times, then make an audio-recording of the performance. (See Tip, left.)

Vocabulary Builder: Country Critters Storyboard

Create a storyboard that extends the story's theme, provides practice with sight words and theme-based vocabulary, and encourages oral language development.

1. Enlarge the Country Critters Storyboard (page 34) and the picture and caption cards (page 35). Color the storyboard and picture cards. Glue the storyboard to tagboard and trim, leaving a border around the scene if desired. Glue the picture and caption cards to tagboard, and cut them apart. Glue an envelope (or resealable bag) to the back of the storyboard. Place picture and caption cards inside.

Tip

Place the book and recording at a center for children to revisit and enjoy on their own. Encourage them to read along with the recording, which will provide many opportunities to practice the phrasing and expression of fluent readers.

Tip

Work with children to write and illustrate a collaborative story about daytime in the country. Encourage them to revisit *Night in the Country* as needed for inspiration, help with phrasing, and reminders about how the author uses sensory language. Use chart paper for the book pages. Then make a cover, bind the pages together to make a big book, and add it to your class library.

2. Model for children how to use the storyboard:

- Remove the picture and caption cards from the envelope. Choose a picture card and say the name for the animal(s). Place the picture card on the storyboard, thinking aloud about where you might see the animal(s)—for example, by the river, in the woods, or in the fields. Find the matching caption card, read the word(s), and place it in the box on the picture card.

- Repeat with other picture and caption cards, using as many as desired on the storyboard.

- When you are finished, use the picture and caption cards to tell a story about animals in the country.

3. Place the storyboard at a center for children to use independently or with partners. NOTE: If desired, make your own picture and caption cards to use with the storyboard. Simply draw or glue pictures of animals on the blank picture cards. Then print a word or phrase on a blank caption card to describe each picture.

Book Links

For more magical looks at country life, share these titles.

- ☼ *In the Garden* by Cynthia Rylant (Atheneum, 1984): This book brings the author and illustrator (Mary Szilagyi) of *Night in the Country* together again for another lustrous look at life in the country. This one follows a family and their garden through the seasons.

- ☼ *Owl Moon* by Jane Yolen (Philomel, 1987): This Caldecott Medal winner captures the wonder of a young girl's nighttime owling adventure on a moonlit winter night in the woods.

- ☼ *Town Mouse, Country Mouse* by Jan Brett (Putnam, 1994): In this twist on a favorite fable, a mouse couple living in town swaps homes with their city-dwelling counterpart. Whether encountering a hungry cat in the city or a predatory owl in the country, each couple discovers they like their own home just fine.

Explore with children how the sights and sounds of night in the country are similar to or different from those for night in the city. Write characteristics of "night" for both locations on index cards. Then create a large Venn diagram and label the circles "Night in the Country" and "Night in the City." Invite children to place the cards on the diagram. When completed, discuss the results: How is night in the country like night in the city? How is it different?

Teaching Reading With Cynthia Rylant Books © 2000 by Jean Newell

an owl	three rabbits	a cow and her calf
two frogs	a dog	a pig
a cat	a raccoon and her babies	a bird

Teaching Reading With Cynthia Rylant Books © 2009 by Joan Novelli, Scholastic Teaching Resources

The Old Woman Who Named Things

(HARCOURT, 1996)

Tip

Consider reading a page or two first before asking children to make a prediction. Often children can make a better prediction after the book is started.

An elderly woman, who has survived all of her friends, decides to name only things she can't outlive. There's Betsy, her trusty old car, and Fred, her sturdy chair. Franklin, her house, is older than she is and still standing strong. She sticks to her rule, even refusing to name a persistent stray puppy because she might outlive him. But when he disappears, she realizes it's worth taking that risk after all.

Before Reading

Share the cover of the book and read aloud the title. Explain that this book is about a woman who names important things in her life. Ask: "Have you every named something special to you?" Guide children to notice details on the cover and predict what sorts of things the woman names. Invite children to share ideas. Then read the first couple of pages and let them revise their predictions.

Tip

Encourage children to make connections to other books by Cynthia Rylant by thinking about similarities between characters, settings, or themes. For example, the woman pictured on the cover of this book might remind them of Miss Maggie, who also lives by herself in the country. Discuss how thinking about what they already know about this author's books can help them make predictions.

During Reading

As you read, pause to reinforce strategies for figuring out unknown words. (You may also read the book through once, then reread to explore new words.) For example, when you read about the woman's chair, Fred, let children explain what they think the author means when she writes that the chair "had never sagged a day in his life." Direct their attention to the picture of the chair to reinforce how illustrations can help them figure out unknown words. Guide students to understand the meaning of the word *sag* (to hang down) and continue reading. Other words that may be new to children include *bumpers* (Which part of the car is the woman cleaning? Where on a car are the bumpers?), *everlasting* (Look at the word parts *ever* and *lasting*; ask: "Why is she reading about everlasting flowers?"), and *kennel* (Use the word *dogcatcher* for a context clue.).

Explore the ways that pictures help readers make sense of a story.

☼ Revisit pages in the book, rereading the text and having students point out details in the illustrations that match up with the words. For example, when the puppy first appears, the text describes a "shy brown puppy" at "the woman's gate." Invite students to explain how the pictures help tell this part of the story.

☼ Explore how illustrations can also provide important information not mentioned in the text. Reread the passage in which the woman first feeds the puppy and tells it to go home. What does the illustration tell children that this text does not? (*The woman is smiling. She probably likes the puppy and is happy to see it. This helps readers predict that the woman will change her mind.*)

Matching the Mood

Explore the way that color in illustrations can evoke feelings or reactions that enhance what's happening in a story. Then let children use what they learn about color and mood to add a new event to the story.

1. Revisit the illustration of the woman driving around looking for the dog and read the text. ("The old woman felt even sadder.")

2. Ask: "What colors do you mostly see in this picture? What kind of a day is it?" Guide children to notice the gray streaks of rain across the page. Ask: "Why do you think the illustrator chose to show a rainy, gray day?" (*It matches the mood in the story; the woman is sad.*)

3. Have children write and illustrate a new "last page" for the story, choosing colors that match the mood of this new event.

4. To go further, create a "Mood Color Chart." Brainstorm words for moods and feelings and write them on chart paper. Discuss which colors best match each mood and add color swatches to the chart accordingly. For example, students might choose yellow for "happy" because it's the color of sunshine. Encourage children to consult the chart for ideas when writing and illustrating their own stories.

Model how you make connections to characters or events in stories to help children understand how thinking about their own experiences can help them better understand a text. In response to the picture of the woman feeding the puppy, you might say, "I remember when a stray cat came to our house, and we fed him. We couldn't find his owners, and every day that he came back we were so excited to see him. He's lived with us for 14 years now! Hmmm. I wonder if she really wants to send that puppy away…"

Plot and Character Go Together

What if the puppy never came along? What if the puppy never went away? Thinking about how events affect a character engages readers in a story and strengthens comprehension, including understanding of cause-and-effect relationships. Use a graphic organizer to help children evaluate how the main character changes as the story moves from beginning to middle to end.

1. Together, recall the main events of the story. Record them on chart paper.

2. Give each child a copy of the reproducible graphic organizer (page 40). Copy it on chart paper and demonstrate how it works: Tell about the beginning, then color in a circle on the scale to show how the woman feels.

3. Have children complete the graphic organizer to keep track of how the woman changes from the beginning to the end of the story.

4. Encourage children to refer to their graphic organizers as you discuss how the woman changes and why.

NOTE: To use this graphic organizer to analyze other ways characters change, mask the labels on the scale and replace with other words that students can use to evaluate how a character changes (for example, *brave* and *scared*).

"Runaway" Sentences

In *Wondrous Words: Writers and Writing in the Elementary Classroom* (NCTE, 1999), Katie Wood Ray writes about the use of "runaway" sentences to "convey a sense of franticness, or desperation, excitement, or being carried away with something." Take a closer look at the text in *The Old Woman Who Named Things* to explore examples of how authors craft these unusual sentences.

1. Reread portions of the text and have students listen for especially long sentences.

2. Choose a long sentence, copy it on chart paper, and read it with students. Here's a fun one to read aloud:

> She told it that Betsy always made puppies sick and Fred never allowed puppies to sit on him and Roxanne wasn't wide enough for a puppy and an old woman to fit on, and besides all this, Franklin couldn't tolerate dog hair.

3. Invite students to share why they think the author made this all one sentence—for example, it helps the reader "hear" the woman tumbling all of her thoughts together as she tries to convince herself that the puppy can't stay. And because there are no commas until the end, readers can almost hear the breath the woman must take just before she makes her final point.

Tip

Let students try out this technique with an interactive writing experience. Choose a highlight from the day that is fresh in students' minds. Together, construct a "runaway" sentence that conveys a feeling of excitement around this event.

4. To go further, children can work with partners to locate "runaway" sentences in other picture books. Read them aloud and discuss the reasons for such long sentences.

Vocabulary Builder: Faces Tell Feelings

This interactive booklet builds on themes in the book to broaden children's vocabulary for words that express different emotions. When you help children build this word knowledge, you give them the tools they need to make more precise connections to story characters and to strengthen their own communication and writing skills.

1. Review words that describe how the woman feels at different points in the story. List the words on chart paper. Let children share other words for feelings and add these to the chart.

2. Give each child several copies of the booklet template (page 41). Copy the rhyme on chart paper and model how to complete it: Read aloud the rhyme, pausing at the blank to fill in a word that names a feeling. Fill in features on the face to show that emotion.

3. Have children complete their pages, add a sheet of blank paper to make a cover, then staple to bind.

4. To go further, have children revisit the Mood Color Chart (see page 37), and color in the backgrounds of their pages to match each feeling.

Book Links

Meet more endearing, elderly characters with stories to tell.

☼ **Little Old Ladies** by Franziska Kalch (Penguin, 2008): No mall-walking or afternoon naps for the "senior" women who star in this story. These dancers, doctors, teachers, and otherwise accomplished women are as lively as the cover illustration pictures them (heading to the finish line in a race!).

☼ **Miss Rumphius** by Barbara Cooney (Viking, 19820): Miss Rumphius lived her life inspired by her grandfather, seeing the world and returning to live by the sea. Satisfied with her life, she still never forgot her grandfather's advice: to "do something to make the world more beautiful." She finally realizes how she can do this, and succeeds in brightening the world wherever she goes with the lupines she loves.

☼ **Wilfred Gordon McDonald Partridge** by Mem Fox (Kane/Miller, 1989): A young boy who lives near a retirement home befriends 96-year-old Miss Nancy and unwittingly helps her recapture special memories.

My face can tell you
A lot about me,
When I'm feeling

This is what you'll see!

Tip

This activity provides a great opportunity to introduce or reinforce use of a thesaurus. When brainstorming and listing words for feelings, ask: "What are some other words that have a similar meaning to this word?" Model how to use a thesaurus to investigate words. For example, children may discover other ways to describe being *happy*, such as *overjoyed*, *delighted*, and *on cloud nine*.

Name _____   Date _____

Book Title: _____

Author: _____

Character: _____

1 **Beginning:** _____

_____

Sad   Happy

2 **Middle:** _____

_____

Sad   Happy

3 **End:** _____

_____

Sad   Happy

Teaching Reading With Cynthia Rylant Books © 2009 by Joan Novelli, Scholastic Teaching Resources

My face can tell you

A lot about me.

When I'm feeling

_____

This is what you'll see!

The Bookshop Dog

(Scholastic/Blue Sky Press, 1996)

People go to Martha Jane's Bookshop for books, of course, but what really brings them in is Martha Jane, the owner's endearing dog. Customers pet her and kiss her and bring her bones. And Martha Jane returns the affection by fetching mail for the mail carrier, making music with the band director, and generally being a pleasant companion to all. So loved was the bookshop dog, that when her owner had to go to the hospital, everyone began to fight over who would take care of Martha Jane. Not surprisingly, Martha Jane chooses the customer with the "Beefy Bone," which leads to a happy ending for all.

Before Reading

Share the cover and invite students to recall other books by Cynthia Rylant that picture a dog on the cover. (There are several, including *When I Was Young in the Mountains*, *The Old Woman Who Named Things*, and *The Great Gracie Chase*.) Point out that the title and cover illustration give readers big clues about the book. Let students tell what those clues are and use them to predict the setting and main character.

During Reading

You'll find many opportunities to "play" with the text and model fluent reading. Although dialogue is limited, there is some between the salesperson, the bookshop owner, and a telephone caller. Use a different voice in each case to help children make sense of who is speaking (and learn to think about the voices of characters in their own reading). Other text features that invite changes in expression and pacing include words in italics, the use of dashes (signaling an aside or extra comment by the author), the layout of text on the page (for example, text that is set off in some way for emphasis, which happens when readers learn about a *most* important decision Martha Jane makes), and the rhythm created by items in a series—sometimes punctuated and sometimes not.

As the problem in the story becomes apparent (Who will take care of Martha Jane when the shop owner goes to the hospital?), take time to remind students to think about what they know about Martha Jane, then make a prediction about what will happen.

Tip

Be sure to share the back flap of the book, which includes a photo of the author and her dog, whose name is also Martha Jane!

Guide a discussion to help students understand the relationship between characters in a story and the plot. Begin by reminding students that the plot is what happens in a story.

- Who is the main character in this story? (*Martha Jane*)

- What words describe Martha Jane? (for example, *good, sweet, helpful*)

- What do people think of Martha Jane? (*They love her.*)

- What happens to create a problem in this story? (*The bookshop owner has to go to the hospital, and everyone wants to take care of Martha Jane.*)

- Considering what you know about Martha Jane, does the ending make sense? (*Yes; Martha Jane is a sweet dog, and everyone wants to help, so readers can predict a happy ending.*)

- If Martha Jane was a difficult dog, do you think things would have happened differently? Why?

Martha Jane's World of Words

Students will probably notice that the illustrations in this colorful book are sprinkled with words. From the name on Martha Jane's bowl to labels on bags of kibble and signs around town, these details add another layer of fun to the story.

1. Invite students to share what they like about the illustrations, including a favorite if they have one.

2. Did students notice all of the words that are part of the illustrations? The dentist's office has a sign, and so, of course, does the bookshop. The doors have "Open" and "Come In" signs, and the shelves have helpful signs for readers looking for mysteries, romances, and . . . dog stories. Children can read the titles on some books, the dog food packaging, even Martha Jane's "Beefy Bone."

3. Send students on a scavenger hunt in the book to locate examples of "environmental print" in Martha Jane's world. Ask questions, such as those that follow, and let students take turns hunting for answers.

   - What shelves would I go to if I wanted to look at mysteries?
   - There's a sign in the bookshop that says "I ♡ books." Who is in the photograph below this sign?
   - What is the name of the hospital the shop owner went to?

(continued)

- What brands of dog food did people bring Martha Jane?
- What's the name of the shop next to the bookshop?
- What kind of book is the shop owner reading in the hospital?
- Who is reading a book called *Easy Pasta Dishes*?
- Who is reading *Read-Aloud Stories*?

Label Makers

Follow up on Martha Jane's World of Words (page 43) with an activity that naturally connects reading and writing at every child's level.

1. Begin by reviewing with students the ways Cynthia Rylant incorporated labels in *The Bookshop Dog* illustrations.

2. Together find examples of labels in the classroom. For example, are learning centers labeled? Bins of crayons, blocks, and puzzles? How about cubbies and cupboards?

3. Provide children with sentence strips (or index cards), crayons, and markers. Let them create labels for areas and items, using words and pictures, then use removable wall adhesive to place them around the room. As in the book, the labels can have single words, phrases, or sentences, and incorporate symbols or pictures (for both visual appeal and word recognition clues).

4. Place a basket of sentence strips, markers, and removable wall adhesive at a writing center to encourage children to create and read more labels.

Vocabulary Builder: *Sweet, Smooth, Good, Green*

Martha Jane is a "good dog," who enjoys a "Beefy Bone," given to her by the "big man in a green coat." Adjectives abound in this colorful book, providing an engaging opportunity to expand vocabulary for descriptive language.

1. In advance, copy a class set of the Word Web template (page 46).

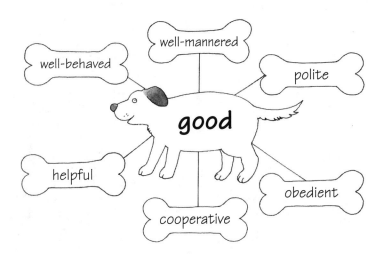

2. Introduce the focus of the lesson by reading a sentence from the book that contains an adjective, for example, "Martha Jane was such a good dog, such a sweet dog." Invite children to identify words in the sentence that describe Martha Jane (*good* and *sweet*). Point out that adjectives are words that describe nouns, in this case *dog*.

3. Revisit other sentences in the book that contain adjectives. Let children practice identifying both the adjectives and the nouns they describe. List adjectives on chart paper and discuss how these types of words help readers make more specific pictures of the text in their minds.

4. Copy the word web onto chart paper and model how to complete it: Choose an adjective from the book (such as *good*) and write it on the dog. Brainstorm other adjectives with a similar meaning and write them on the bones. (See sample, above.)

5. Give each child a copy of the word web. Have children choose an adjective from the chart to write on the dog and then generate a group of related adjectives to complete the web.

Book Links

Meet more irresistible pets with these stories.

☼ *Crictor* by Tomi Ungerer (HarperCollins, 1983): In this Reading Rainbow selection, Crictor is a boa constrictor who lives with Madame Bodot in a French village, where he proves to be a helpful pet in all sorts of ways.

☼ *I Wanna Iguana* by Karen Kaufman (Putnam, 2004): In this perfect lesson on persuasive writing, a boy exchanges notes with his mother, as he tries to convince her to let him adopt his friend's iguana.

☼ *Martha Speaks* by Susan Meddaugh (Houghton Mifflin, 1992): After devouring a bowl of alphabet soup, Martha suddenly speaks nonstop. Speech balloons add another layer to the story, with Martha's comments providing much amusement.

Name _____

Date _____

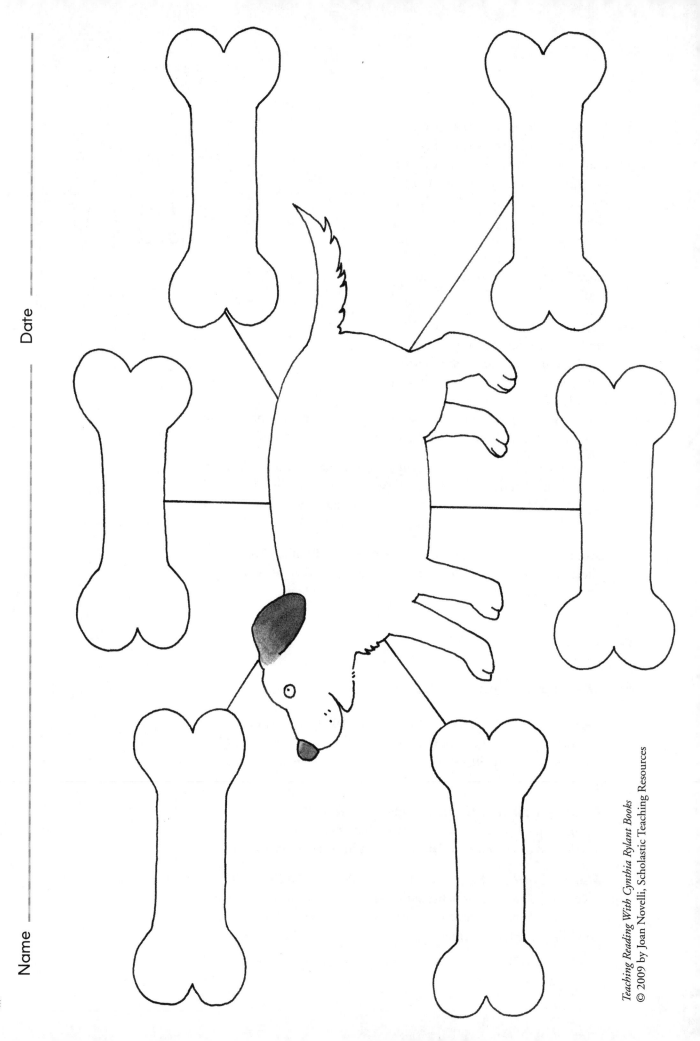

Teaching Reading With Cynthia Rylant Books
© 2009 by Joan Novelli, Scholastic Teaching Resources

In November

(Harcourt, 2000)

"In November, the earth is growing quiet. It is making its bed, a winter bed for flowers and small creatures…" As birds fly away, the "air is full of good-byes." Cats cuddle and families gather in thanks, in the month that "tastes like cinnamon." With poetic text and richly textured paintings, each page in this cozy book captures something special about this autumn month.

Before Reading

Without showing the title, take a picture walk through the book. Invite children to predict what the book is about and guess what the title might be. Then, reveal the title and let children share what they know about this time of year.

During Reading

Invite children to imagine that they are "in the story." As you read aloud each page, encourage them to use their senses to feel, for example, the chilly air that makes the animals shiver, or the warmth of the soft, furry cats as they snuggle together in the barn. Pause to model how you use your senses, too, to support students in actively "experiencing" the story. You might say, for example, "I wonder what the author means about November being an 'orange smell.' A pumpkin is orange, and I can imagine the smell of a pumpkin pie baking. It smells like cinnamon, ginger, cloves, and nutmeg. Mmmmm. I can almost taste it!"

After Reading

In *Growing Readers* (Stenhouse, 1964), Kathy Collins discusses strategies for picturing what's happening in a story, such as "imagine the behind-the-scenes things that are going on." Revisit several passages to practice this engaging comprehension strategy. (For a follow up, see A Snapshot in Time and Life Under Snow, page 48.)

✧ Readers learn that small creatures are hiding in a "winter bed." Ask: "If you could look under the snow in this picture, what do you think you'd find?" (*insects, spiders, mice, and other rodents*)

✧ For birds in winter, berries are "treasures." Ask: "What other food might 'staying birds' find?" (for example, *seeds in bird feeders*)

(continued)

Tip

To enhance children's understanding of the "pumpkin smell" that "tastes like cinnamon and can fill up a house," bring in some pumpkin pie spice blend (or cinnamon, ginger, cloves, and nutmeg). Place the spice mixture in several shallow containers. Let children smell the spices and imagine a pumpkin pie baking as you reread the passage.

☀ The farmer is carrying a bucket. Ask: "Where do you think the farmer is going? How is he getting the barn ready for winter?" (For example, *he may check to make sure the barn will be warm, that the animals have extra bedding and food, and that the water supply is protected from freezing.*)

A Snapshot in Time

Stretch children's comprehension skills with an activity that looks at illustrations from a photographer's point of view.

1. The series of illustrations beginning with the dogs in front of the fire can easily be imagined as photos of a family get-together. Choose a series of several snapshots that picture a similar event (or a classroom activity) and show children one that occurs at some point in the middle. Together, "read" the photo by answering "Who," "What," "When," "Where," and "Why" questions.

2. Explain that a photo captures a single moment in time, but that something is always happening before and after. Let children guess what the subjects in the photo were doing before and after that moment, then share those photos.

3. Choose an illustration in the book, such as the one that pictures the dogs in front of a fire. Apply the same procedure with this illustration, inviting children to "read" it by answering the five "wh" questions and then explaining what the before and after snapshots might show. For example, children might imagine that before the dogs settled down by the fire, they were playing outside. An "after" picture might have captured them barking at the door as guests arrived.

4. Repeat with other pictures in the book. As children practice this strategy, they'll more actively engage in the story and deepen their understanding.

Life Under Snow

Create an interactive mural that involves students in researching what happens beneath a blanket of snow and inspires storytelling that strengthens oral language development.

1. Set up a KWL chart (What We Know, What We Want to Know, What We Learned). Revisit the illustration of earth's "winter bed" and have students share what they know about life under the snow. Add this information to the chart (K), then invite students to wonder what other activity might take place under the snow (W). Together, research the topic and record new information (L). Try to gather a fact for every student or pair.

2. Display a sheet of mural paper and, together, create a basic framework for the scene—for example, draw several winter trees, a berry bush, geese,

and a blanket of snow. Be sure to leave plenty of room to depict life under the snow.

3. Have each student (or pair) choose one fact to illustrate on the mural. On index cards, have students write (or dictate) a sentence to go with their picture.

4. Place the fact cards and removable wall adhesive in a basket near the mural. Let children use the fact cards to label the mural and tell a behind-the-scenes story about winter life under a bed of snow.

Special Months Mini-Book

Reinforce concepts in the book related to cycles and seasons with "layer" books children create to celebrate a month that is special to them. These easy-to-make books feature predictable text patterns (based on *In November*) that visually repeat from one layer to the next, building word recognition and success into the reading experience.

1. For each book, layer five sheets of paper as shown (right). Fold the top down to meet the bottom and staple to bind. This will create a layer book with a cover and four "pages" for students to complete.

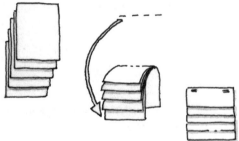

2. Have children choose a month that is special to them. Model how to complete the book:

- Using *In November* as a model, write a title on the cover page and illustrate it.
- On the exposed section of each "layer," write (or dictate) a sentence about the selected month. Begin each sentence with "In [name of month]"—for example, "In September, it is my birthday."
- Lift the overlapping page and draw a picture above the sentence.

3. As children complete their books, guide them to notice that the same words begin each sentence and are lined up on the layers. Also, point out how their pictures match words in their sentences. Explain that readers use picture clues to help figure out unknown words.

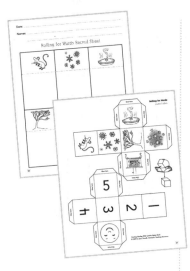

Vocabulary Builder: Rolling for Words

In November, "the air is chilly…" and the animals "shiver." Cats pile up to stay warm, and a woodstove crackles. Expand children's vocabulary with a game that promotes creative thinking, nurtures a curiosity for language, and builds a growing bank of descriptive words.

1. In advance, make a set of game cubes (page 51) and copy the record sheet (page 52) for each group of 3–4 students. Color the cubes if desired.

2. Divide the class into small groups. Give each group a set of game cubes, a record sheet, and a pencil. Point out that one game cube has numbers on it, and the other has story pictures. Review the pictures and invite children to recall words from the story that describe each picture, such as *small* (mouse), *crackling* (woodstove), *lovely* (trees), and *brittle* (stars). Then model how to play:

   - Roll the game cubes. Say the name for the picture and number—for example, "mouse" and "3."

   - Name that number of words to describe the picture—for example, for *mouse*, the player might suggest *small*, *tiny*, and *little*. Other players can help with words if asked. Players may also consult a thesaurus. If the number cube lands on the smiley face, everyone in the group helps to name as many words as they can to describe the picture.

   - Write the words under the appropriate picture on the record sheet.

   - Continue playing until each picture has been rolled at least once.

3. Bring the groups together to share the words on their record sheets. Then compile the words on a wall chart.

Book Links

Compare *In November* to other books about autumn.

- *Every Autumn Comes the Bear* by Jim Arnosky (Putnam, 1996): Beginning with a bear that seems to step right out of the cover, this story captures the imposing creature's presence in the woods as he looks for a place to settle in for the winter.

- *Leaf Man* by Lois Ehlert (Harcourt, 2005): In this fanciful look at fall, leaves from different trees take the shape of animals and objects.

- *'Twas the Night Before Thanksgiving* by Dav Pilkey (Orchard, 1990): A field trip to a turkey farm leads to a turkey rescue and a nontraditional Thanksgiving feast of "veggies with jelly and toast."

Tip

Modify the picture cube to reinforce descriptive words in other stories or to generate new words. To do this, mask the pictures on the cube and replace them with new pictures related to this story or another one.

Glue here.

Glue here.

Glue here.

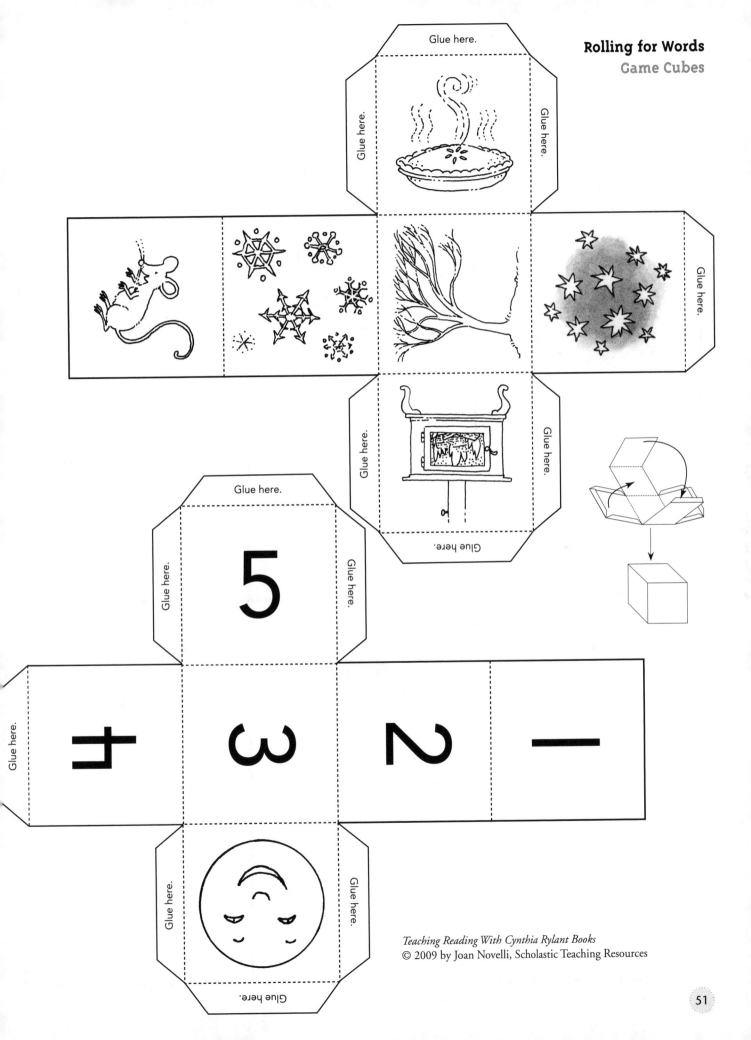

Glue here.

Glue here.

Glue here.

Glue here.

Glue here.

Glue here.

5

4

3

2

1

Glue here.

Glue here.

Glue here.

Glue here.

Teaching Reading With Cynthia Rylant Books
© 2009 by Joan Novelli, Scholastic Teaching Resources

Date: _____

Names: _____   _____

_____   _____

Rolling for Words Record Sheet

Teaching Reading With Cynthia Rylant Books © 2009 by Joan Novelli, Scholastic Teaching Resources

The Great Gracie Chase: Stop That Dog!

(SCHOLASTIC/BLUE SKY PRESS, 2001)

Little Gracie Rose enjoys her quiet life, with "the kitty sleeping on the windowsill, the big dog sleeping on the couch, the quiet fish going ploop-ploop." So when the painters come in their "big, noisy truck," Gracie barks in displeasure and is promptly placed outside. Out the gate she goes, and the Great Gracie Chase begins. Comical, slightly askew illustrations by Mark Teague get readers right in on the action.

Before Reading

Share the cover and read the title. Point out the exclamation at the end of the title. Invite students to read the title with you, putting emphasis on "Stop That Dog!" Then have them look at the illustration and predict what might happen in this story. Invite students to compare this book with other books by Cynthia Rylant. They might recall other books that picture a dog on the cover, such as *When I Was Young in the Mountains*, *The Old Woman Who Named Things*, and *The Bookshop Dog*. They might also notice that the cover illustration is more cartoon-like, suggesting that the story might be sillier than some of Rylant's other books.

During Reading

"THERE'S GRACIE!" Take advantage of text features (including uppercase words, italicized text, ellipses, and parenthetical text) to model reading with expression. Point to the text as you read so students can match the text features they see with the expression in your voice. Students will learn that reading with expression adds interest and meaning to a story and helps them understand what's happening. (For an activity that takes a closer look at text features, see Tip, page 54.)

After Reading

This story is a natural for teaching cause-and-effect relationships, which helps readers better understand characters and make sense of the plot. Introduce the terms *cause* (why something happens) and *effect* (what happens as a result). Then, to help children recognize cause-and-effect relationships in the story and develop vocabulary that signals these relationships (such as *when*, *so*, *because*, and *since*), read each of the following sentence-starters, inserting a cause-and-effect signal word at the end. Invite a volunteer to complete the sentence, then repeat with a new signal word.

(continued)

Revisit the story and point out words that are in uppercase letters, italic type, or both. Ask: "What does the way these words look tell us about the feeling the author wants to express? How does this help us know how to read these words?" Read a few examples in a "plain" voice, followed by a "loud" voice that matches the text. Discuss how your expression helps tell the story. Finally, reread the story and let children join in on words in uppercase letters.

❖ Gracie started barking (*because, when, so*) _____ .

❖ The painters put Gracie outside (*because, when, so*) _____ .

❖ Gracie didn't like being put outside (*so, because*) _____ .

❖ Gracie started running (*when, because, so*) _____ .

❖ People were chasing Gracie (*because, so*) _____ .

❖ Gracie kept running (*so, because, since*) _____ .

❖ Everybody stopped chasing Gracie (*when, so, because*) _____ .

❖ Gracie walked back home (*when, since*) _____ .

Read Around the Town

From Bob the Painter's truck to the hot dog cart, signs around Gracie's town are a fun extra in this story. Long before they can read books, children can read environmental print—the signs and symbols in the world around them. From cereal boxes to banners on buses and stop signs, environmental print provides young children with daily opportunities to build literacy skills. Create an easy-to-make book featuring familiar environmental print to provide reading practice and celebrate children's growing reading skills.

1. Revisit pages in the book and have children locate the signs in different scenes, beginning with the painters' truck: BOB'S PAINTING "WE DO OUR BEST." Invite children to read any words they can using what they know about letters and sounds, as well as picture clues.

2. Share examples of environmental print, such as pictures of safety signs, photos of signs around town (traffic signs, shops, and so on), and logos, such as those from cereal boxes and milk cartons. Invite children to read the words with you and share others they know.

3. Over a period of a week or so, have children bring to school examples of print in the world around them. (Send home a letter letting families know what sorts of things children can bring in.)

4. Give children a sheet of paper. Have each child choose one sample to glue on the paper and then draw additional art, if desired. (Have extra samples on hand for students who need one.) Put the pages together, add a cover, then staple to bind.

5. Read the book together, letting children share pages they've contributed. Then place the book in the class library for children to read again and again.

What's All the Barking About?

Gracie barks, but if she could talk, what would she say? Revisit dialogue in the story and let students add some of their own to learn more about how this text feature works.

1. Use an example from the book to introduce dialogue, such as:

   "Stop that dog!" everybody cried.

   Copy the sentence on chart paper. Let volunteers identify the punctuation (quotation marks) that encloses the speaker's words and the dialogue tag that tells who is speaking. Read aloud the dialogue and point out how it helps readers picture being in the crowd of townspeople as they chase Gracie. Ask children to look for other examples of dialogue in the book to reinforce recognition of this text feature.

2. Revisit the beginning of the story, when Gracie barks at the noisy painters. Ask: "What do you think Gracie is trying to tell the painters?" Invite a volunteer to speak for Gracie and write the words on the chart paper. Have the child place quotation marks around the words that Gracie says, and add (or dictate) a dialogue tag. Reread this part of the story, substituting the new dialogue for text that tells about Gracie barking.

3. Have students pair up to create dialogue for Gracie to go with a favorite part of the story. For example, as Gracie is put outside, their dialogue might read:

   "I don't like this one bit," Gracie complained.

   Have students write (or dictate) the dialogue on a large sticky note, then practice reading it aloud to get Gracie's "voice" just right.

4. Place students' sticky notes on the corresponding pages, then reread the story, letting children read their dialogue in place of the actual text.

Vocabulary Builder: Bark, Walk, Run!

Gracie's walk quickly turned into a run—down the street, up the hill, across the schoolyard, and through the fountain. Use the many action verbs in this story as a springboard for a mini-lesson on present- and past-tense verbs. Learning to recognize suffixes such as those used to form past-tense verbs helps children develop strategies (such as identifying base words) for figuring out challenging vocabulary they encounter in their own reading.

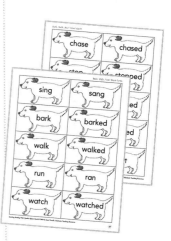

1. To prepare, copy and cut apart the word cards (pages 57–58).

(continued)

2. Introduce the lesson by reminding children what action verbs are (words that tell what someone or something is doing). Invite children to name action words from the story and list them on chart paper.

3. Use the words to discuss present- and past-tense verbs. Which words tell what is happening now? Which words tell what has already happened?

4. Demonstrate different ways to form past-tense words. For example, for *walk*, add the ending *-ed* (*walked*). For other words, such as *stop*, double the final consonant and add *-ed* (*stopped*). Point out irregular past-tense verbs, such as *run*, and explain how the spelling changes (*ran*).

5. Use the cards in any of the following ways to provide practice with present- and past-tense verbs.

   - **Mingle and Match:** Give each child a card. Depending on the number of children, you may need to create extra sets of cards. (See additional verb pairs, left.) Make sure each child has a word from a matched pair. Then invite children to mingle, looking for the classmate with the matching verb. Have children then use their words to retell part of the story (in both present and past tense).

   - **Now and Then:** Place the cards at a center with two trays or paper plates labeled "Now" and "Then." Have children sort the cards accordingly as they read them.

   - **Pocket-Chart Fill-Ins:** To create a pocket-chart activity, write events from the story on sentence strips, one sentence per strip. In place of the verbs, draw a box sized to fit the cards. Number the sentence strips on the back to assist children with sequencing. Model how to sequence the sentences and use the cards to fill in the blanks. Then let children work together in pairs to do the same.

Additional Present- and Past-Tense Verb Pairs

catch	caught
*try	tried
*cry	cried
watch	watched
trip	tripped
fall	fell
think	thought

*You might teach dropping the *y* and adding *i*.

Book Links

Meet more dogs with personalities as big as Gracie's.

☼ *Dear Mrs. LaRue: Letters From Obedience School* by Mark Teague (Scholastic, 2002): Ike, a disobedient dog whose owner sends him off to the Canine Academy, launches a comical letter-writing campaign aimed at getting his owner to reconsider.

☼ *Officer Buckle and Gloria* by Peggy Rathman (Putnam, 1995): Officer Buckle finally gets his safety message across to kids at schools—with the help of his police dog, Gloria.

☼ *Pinkerton, Behave!* by Stephen Kellogg (Dial, 2002): This is part of the popular series that chronicles the adventures of a playful and slightly unmanageable Great Dane.

sing

sang

bark

barked

walk

walked

run

ran

watch

watched

chase

chased

stop

stopped

look

looked

rest

rested

leave

left

Poppleton

(Scholastic/Blue Sky Press, 1997)

In the first installment of this favorite beginning-reader chapter book series, readers meet Poppleton, a polite pig who has relocated from the city to a small town. Poppleton settles into his new home and gets to know two of his new neighbors, a well-meaning llama named Cherry Sue and a goat named Fillmore. These characters reappear throughout the series, as readers meet other dear friends, including Hudson (a mouse), Patrick (a finch), Gus (the mail-carrier tortoise), and Newhouse (the delivery dog). Mark Teague's expressive illustrations are filled with humorous details.

> Use the suggestions on pages 59–65 with any Poppleton book to support your reading program.

Before Reading

Preview the cover of the book of your choice in this series. Ask questions to guide children in thinking about what they know and making predictions.

- What words in the title help you predict what will happen in the story?

- Who do you see on the cover? Have you seen these characters before? What do you already know about them?

- What is Poppleton doing? (or, Where do you think he's going?)

- Do you think the characters will have fun? What are some clues?

- What do you think will happen in this story? (Encourage students to think about other plot patterns in Poppleton books they've read.)

During Reading

As you read the books in this series, use the following routines to guide students in using comprehension strategies.

- **Notice Chapter Titles:** Share the contents page and explain how this text feature helps readers. Make a connection to other texts that have a contents page, such as nonfiction books. As you read, point out the chapter titles at the beginning of each chapter. Ask: "How does reading the chapter title help you predict what this part of the story will be about?"

- **"Listen" to Characters:** The Poppleton books are filled with expressive, playful dialogue. Let students know that readers think about how a character might sound. Vary your voice when reading to demonstrate

Books in the Poppleton Series

These warm, witty books explore themes of friendship, neighborhood, and manners, making them easily relatable to a range of classroom lessons. The series includes the following titles:

- *Poppleton*
- *Poppleton and Friends*
- *Poppleton Everyday*
- *Poppleton Forever*
- *Poppleton in Spring*
- *Poppleton in Fall*
- *Poppleton Has Fun*
- *Poppleton in Winter*

(continued)

By noticing how authors write dialogue, children can better understand characters and events, and they can also learn how they might choose more precise words in their own writing. Point out that in the Poppleton series, the characters don't always just "say" their words—often they roar, yell, shout, croak, cry, or call their words. Invite children to hunt for words that tell how a character is speaking. Write each verb on a speech bubble and display the bubbles. Encourage children to use the display as a reference for their own writing.

how this works. For example, Poppleton is a well-mannered pig, so it makes sense that he speaks politely (except when he's frustrated or worried, in which case words in uppercase letters are a sure sign about how he sounds). For a related activity, see Tip, left.

- **Ask Questions:** Encourage children to ask questions based on events to confirm or revise predictions, figure out something new, and check understanding. For example, when Poppleton soaks Cherry Sue with the hose (in *Poppleton*), children might wonder, "What will Cherry Sue do about this?" When she laughs instead of getting upset, readers might confirm an earlier prediction that Poppleton and Cherry Sue will be friends. They also learn something about her personality: She is good-natured. After reading this first chapter, students can pause and ask themselves: Does this make sense? Poppleton and Cherry Sue had fun at first, and then they had a problem. But they solved their problem, so it makes sense that they're now friends.

- **Make Connections:** Have students pause at a point in each chapter to make connections to specific events. For example, in "The Pill" (*Poppleton*), children can relate to Poppleton when he is sick in bed: How do they feel when they're sick? Cake makes Poppleton feel better. What makes them feel better?

After Reading

Ask questions to check comprehension. The following questions are based on *Poppleton*. Adapt the questions for use with other books in the series.

- **Draw Conclusions:** Why does Cherry Sue offer Poppleton oatmeal, toasted cheese, and spaghetti every day? (*She is just being kind to her new neighbor.*)

- **Make Inferences:** When Poppleton goes to the library, why does he always have a table to himself? (*Reading is very important to him, so he doesn't want to be disturbed.*)

- **Recall Details:** What does Poppleton always bring to the library? (*He brings his eyeglasses, tissues, lip balm, pocket watch, book marker, and duffel.*)

What's on the Walls?

A picture might not be worth quite 1,000 words, but the illustrations in the Poppleton books do much to enhance and expand on the text, with clever details that readers will continue to uncover each time they revisit a book. Take a closer look at one recurring element in the illustrations: the paintings that adorn various characters' walls. Then let students take a turn as illustrator and add one more picture to a favorite character's walls.

1. Invite students to describe paintings or pictures they see at school, in their homes, or in other places they've been, such as a bank, doctor's office, or library. Ask: "How do people decide what sorts of pictures to hang on their walls?" Guide students to recognize that people often display family photos and pictures of favorite places or things.

2. Point out that students may have noticed the paintings hanging in the homes of the Poppleton characters. Browse books for examples, such as the following:

   - *Poppleton*: portraits of Cherry Sue (Cherry Sue's home) and a picture of a tin can (Fillmore's home)
   - *Poppleton and Friends*: a grouping of paintings, including a fish, a sailboat, and a shore scene (Poppleton's home)
   - *Poppleton Everyday:* ice cream sundae, with cake and donuts (Poppleton's home)
   - *Poppleton Forever*: hamburger (Poppleton's home; also note the wallpaper covered in ice cream sundaes and cupcakes!)

3. Discuss what the pictures tell readers about the characters (and why they're funny). Then invite students to choose a favorite character and, using what they know, create a new painting to "hang" in that character's home. For example, a student might paint a group portrait of all of Poppleton's friends to show how important they are to him. Another might paint a (mouse-size) picture of cheese.

4. Invite students to "frame" their paintings on slightly larger sheets of colored paper. (They might also write a sentence that tells which character the painting is for and why.) Group students' work by character and display on a bulletin board or wall. If possible, back the bulletin board or wall space for each grouping in paper that relates to each character.

Tip

Copy compound words from the Poppleton series onto sentence strips. Cut apart the strips to separate the two word parts. Then mix up the cards, give one to each student (be sure there's a match for each child), and have students find the classmate whose word matches. When all the matches have been found, invite partners to identify the compound word made with their two words and to tell its meaning. Here are some compound words from the Poppleton series:

armload	overflowing
birthday	pancakes
bluebird	sailboat
doorbell	saleslady
eyeglasses	stargazed
grapefruit	sunroom
landlocked	thumbtacks
oatmeal	wallpaper
outside	

Sight-Word Sidewalk Game

Play a game that revisits favorite story scenes and provides the sight-word practice children need to become independent readers.

1. For each group of 3–4 players, copy and cut out the following materials:

   - game directions (page 62)
   - game board (page 63)
   - game cards (page 64)
   - number pyramid and game markers (page 65)

   (continued)

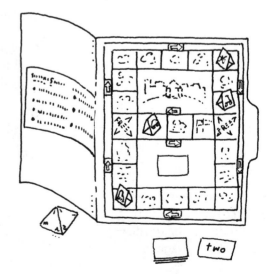

2. Color the game board and glue it to the right side of an open file folder. Glue the directions to the left side. Then tape a resealable plastic bag to the back of the file folder (only the sides and bottom of the bag). Have children color the game markers. Assemble the markers and number pyramid (as shown). Place the game cards, markers, and number pyramid in the bag.

3. Review the word cards and directions with students before they play.

Sight-Word Sidewalk Game • Directions

1 Each player places a game marker on a different corner space on the game board.

2 Shuffle the cards and deal four to each player. Stack the remaining cards facedown on the game board.

3 To take a turn, roll the number pyramid. Move that number of spaces. Follow the arrows.

4 Look for a card in your hand that helps tell about the picture on the space. (Examples: *a* garden, *the* car, *three* bikes, birds *in* a tree.) You may have more than one word you can use. Choose only one card to play. Read that word and use it to tell about the picture, then place the card to the side.

5 If you do not have a card that helps tell about the picture, take the top card from the stack. Try to use the card to name the picture. If you can't, return the card to the bottom of the stack, and your turn ends.

6 If you land on a "FREE!" space, you may use any of your cards to tell about a picture on any space on the game board.

7 Continue playing until one player is out of cards or all of the cards have been used.

Playing Tips:

- Players may land on and share the same space.
- Players may move around the game board as many times as needed.
- Players may move in either direction when taking the shortcut.

Book Links

Meet more pigs, including some real ones.

☼ *Life on a Pig Farm* by Judy Wolfman (Carolrhoda, 2001): In this appealing photo-essay, readers meet a young girl who raises pigs on her family's farm.

☼ *Pigs* by Gail Gibbons (Holiday House, 2000): Simple text and cheerful watercolor illustrations provide information on this favorite farm animal.

☼ *Snuffles and Snouts* selected by Laura Robb (Puffin, 1999): This collection of pig poems includes selections by Ogden Nash, Myra Cohn Livingston, and Mary Ann Hoberman.

☼ *Those Can-Do Pigs* by David McPhail (Dutton, 1996): The energetic friends from the popular *Pigs Aplenty, Pigs Galore!* (Dutton, 1993) have returned to lend a helping hoof to others.

Tip

For more activities to use with the Poppleton series, see Tips for Teaching With Chapter Books (pages 11–13).

Sight-Word Sidewalk Game

Place cards here.

a	four	on	there
and	full	one	this
are	has	some	those
at	in	ten	three
by	is	that	two
five	it	the	with

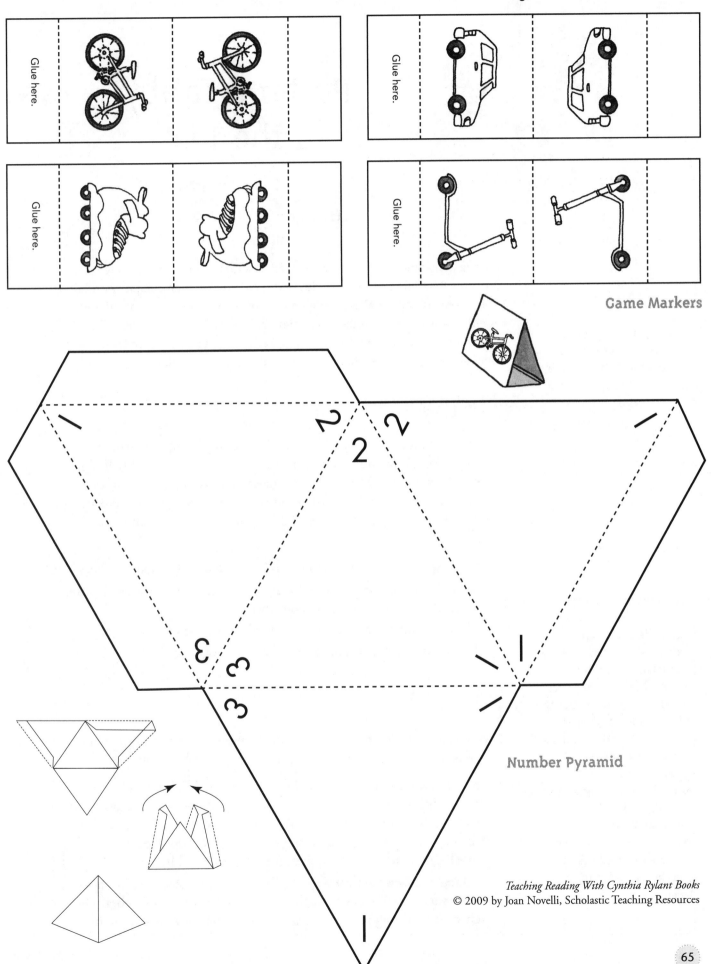

Glue here.

Glue here.

Glue here.

Glue here.

Game Markers

Number Pyramid

Teaching Reading With Cynthia Rylant Books
© 2009 by Joan Novelli, Scholastic Teaching Resources

Mr. Putter & Tabby
Pour the Tea

(HARCOURT, 1994)

I n the first volume of this charming series, Mr. Putter has stories to tell, but no one to tell them to. He decides that a cat will be good company and finds Tabby at the animal shelter. In the books that follow, they enjoy a series of everyday adventures together that often include their next-door neighbor Mrs. Teaberry and her "lollypup" of a dog, Zeke. Young readers will enjoy finding funny details tucked into delightful illustrations by Arthur Howard.

Before Reading

Children will quickly become familiar with the predictable text structure in the titles ("*Mr. Putter and Tabby…*") and the characters pictured (Mr. Putter, Tabby, and sometimes Mrs. Teaberry and her dog, Zeke). As you preview the cover of a new book, invite children to read words they recognize. Ask questions like the following to guide them in thinking about what they know and in making predictions.

- What words in the title help you predict what will happen in this story?
- Who do you see on the cover? Have you seen these characters before? What do you already know about them?
- What do you think Mr. Putter and Tabby will do in this story?
- Do you think these characters will have fun together? How do you know?

During Reading

As you read the books in this series, guide students in practicing comprehension strategies, beginning with using a table of contents.

- **Notice Chapter Titles:** Share the contents page and explain how this text feature helps readers. Make a connection to other texts that have a contents page, such as nonfiction books. As you read, point out the same chapter titles at the beginning of each chapter. Ask: "How does reading the chapter title help you predict what this part of the story will be about?"
- **"Listen" to Characters:** Readers get to know the characters in the Mr. Putter and Tabby series through narrative (what we are told about the characters), dialogue (words that the characters say, in quotation marks),

Use the suggestions on pages 66–71 with any Mr. Putter & Tabby book to support your reading program.

Tip

Part of the fun of reading books in a series is the way certain details reappear every now and then. The characters and setting become like old friends, and this sense of familiarity allows readers to deepen their understanding. Set up a chart for keeping track of repeating details. For example, there is the striped chair in front of the window where Mr. Putter sits with Tabby every evening, the hammock where he rests, and the tea and muffins he enjoys.

and details in the illustrations that help them figure out what the characters are thinking and feeling. Look for opportunities to explore this with students. For example, they can imagine that Mr. Putter has a gentle, kind voice because the author tells readers that he has "a very soft heart." (*Mr. Putter and Tabby Walk the Dog*) But when Mrs. Teaberry's dog tugs and chases and wraps Mr. Putter around trees, the illustrations provide clues about how he sounds when he declares Zeke "a nightmare."

☼ **Ask Questions:** Encourage children to ask questions to check predictions and figure out something new. For example, they can predict from the cover of *Mr. Putter & Tabby Bake the Cake* that Mr. Putter is going to bake a cake. Judging from his expression, they can also guess that he doesn't know how to bake a cake, and that this will cause some problems. When the text confirms that he doesn't know how, students can ask: "What will Mr. Putter do now?" Just as they predicted, Mr. Putter has some cake-baking disasters. And in the way that he handles these problems, students also discover that Mr. Putter has determination.

☼ **Make Connections:** The characters' everyday adventures make it easy for students to relate to these stories. For example, in *Mr. Putter & Tabby Fly the Plane*, they learn that Mr. Putter loves visiting the toy store, where he plays with everything, but mostly the planes. Students can make connections to their own favorite toys.

More Adventures With Mr. Putter and Tabby

Other titles in this beginning reader series include:

- *Mr. Putter & Tabby Pour the Tea*
- *Mr. Putter & Tabby Walk the Dog*
- *Mr. Putter & Tabby Bake the Cake*
- *Mr. Putter & Tabby Pick the Pears*
- *Mr. Putter & Tabby Fly the Plane*
- *Mr. Putter & Tabby Row the Boat*
- *Mr. Putter & Tabby Toot the Horn*
- *Mr. Putter & Tabby Take the Train*
- *Mr. Putter & Tabby Paint the Porch*
- *Mr. Putter & Tabby Feed the Fish*
- *Mr. Putter & Tabby Catch the Cold*
- *Mr. Putter & Tabby Stir the Soup*
- *Mr. Putter & Tabby Write the Book*
- *Mr. Putter & Tabby Make a Wish*
- *Mr. Putter & Tabby Spin the Yarn*
- *Mr. Putter & Tabby Run the Race*
- *Mr. Putter & Tabby See the Stars*
- *Mr. Putter & Tabby Drop the Ball*
- *Mr. Putter & Tabby Spill the Beans*

After Reading

 Check students' understanding with questions that revisit the story on different levels—from recalling details to expressing opinions. The following suggestions are based on *Mr. Putter & Tabby Pour the Tea*, but can be adapted for use with other books in the series.

☼ **Recall Details:** How does Mr. Putter spend his days? (*tending to his flowers and trees*)

☼ **Make an Inference:** What kind of a book is Mr. Putter looking at? What kinds of stories do you think he likes to tell? (*a photo album; memories from his life*)

☼ **Understand Story Structure:** What problem is Mr. Putter trying to solve? How does he solve that problem? (*Mr. Putter is lonely; he decides to get a cat for company.*)

☼ **Draw Conclusions:** Do you think Mr. Putter will be happy with Tabby? What are some clues? (*Answers will vary.*)

☼ **Evaluate:** What did you think was the funniest part of this story? Why? (*Answers will vary.*)

Tip

For more suggestions for teaching with the Mr. Putter & Tabby series, see Tips for Teaching With Chapter Books (pages 11–13).

Word-Family Sort

The titles in this series feature words that make great starting points for teaching word families. This game provides practice with eight book-based, short- and long-vowel phonograms, and is easily adapted for others. (See blank picture and word card templates, page 71.)

1. For each group of 3–4 players, prepare the following materials:

   - Copy and cut out the game directions (below).

   - Make a copy of the Word-Family Sort game board for each player (page 70). Glue each game board to tagboard and trim to size.

   - Copy, color, and cut apart a set of picture cards (page 70).

   - Copy and cut apart a set of word cards (page 71).

   - Copy and cut out the number pyramid template (page 65). Follow directions for assembly.

   - For storage, place all the materials for each game in a resealable plastic bag.

2. After preparing the game, review the directions to show children how to play.

Word-Family Sort • Directions

1 Each player chooses two picture cards. Place them in the boxes at the top of the game board.

2 Mix up the word cards and stack them facedown. (Use only those word cards that go with the picture cards on players' boards. For four players, use all of the word cards. For fewer players, set aside the extra cards.)

3 To take a turn, roll the number pyramid. Take that number of word cards.

4 Read each word. If it rhymes with the name of one of your pictures, place it in a box under that picture. If not, return the card to the bottom of the stack, and your turn ends.

5 Continue playing until one player fills his or her game board (or until all players fill their game board).

Snapshot Stories

In *Mr. Putter & Tabby Pour the Tea*, students see Mr. Putter paging through a photo album as he recalls stories from his life. What memories will he make with Tabby? Create new "photo album" pages to help children sequence important events in each book.

1. Share a page from a photo album (such as one from a class field trip) that shows a sequence of events—for example, getting on the bus, arriving at the apple orchard, picking apples, and making applesauce. Discuss with children how the photos help them recall important events in order.

2. Give each child a sheet of 11- by 14-inch paper and four 4- by 6-inch sheets of paper.

3. Invite children to create a new page for Mr. Putter's photo album. On the 4- by 6-inch papers, have them draw four "photos" that represent important events in a story from beginning to end. Have them glue their photos in order to the larger sheet of paper, and add small triangles of black or white paper to make "photo corners." Children can write simple captions to summarize each event.

4. Let children pair up to share their "photo album" pages and use their pictures to retell the story. Reinforce the use of time-order words in retellings, such as *first*, *then*, *next*, and *finally*.

Book Links

Meet more fabulous felines in these books.

☼ *Hi, Cat!* by Ezra Jack Keats (Macmillan, 1970): A stray cat follows Archie and disrupts the show he is putting on for his friends. After a frustrating day, Archie discovers that the cat may not be so bad after all.

☼ *Millions of Cats* by Wanda Gag (Penguin, 1928): This Newbery Honor favorite tells the story of a man who sets out to find a pet—and returns home with "millions and billions and trillions of cats."

☼ *Wabi Sabi* by Mark Reibstein (Little Brown, 2008): Richly textured illustrations accompany this unusual story about a cat in Japan who goes on a quest to uncover the meaning of her name.

Tip

Tabby's expressions tell readers a lot about what she's thinking and feeling. And when she purrs, readers know she is content. Brainstorm words for animal sounds, such as *screech* (owl), *snort* (rhinoceros), and *squeak* (mouse). Let each child choose an animal sound and create an illustrated word card. Display the word cards to create a lively wall chart. When you have a few minutes during a transition time, read the words with children, inviting them to say each word in the "voice" of the animal that makes that sound.

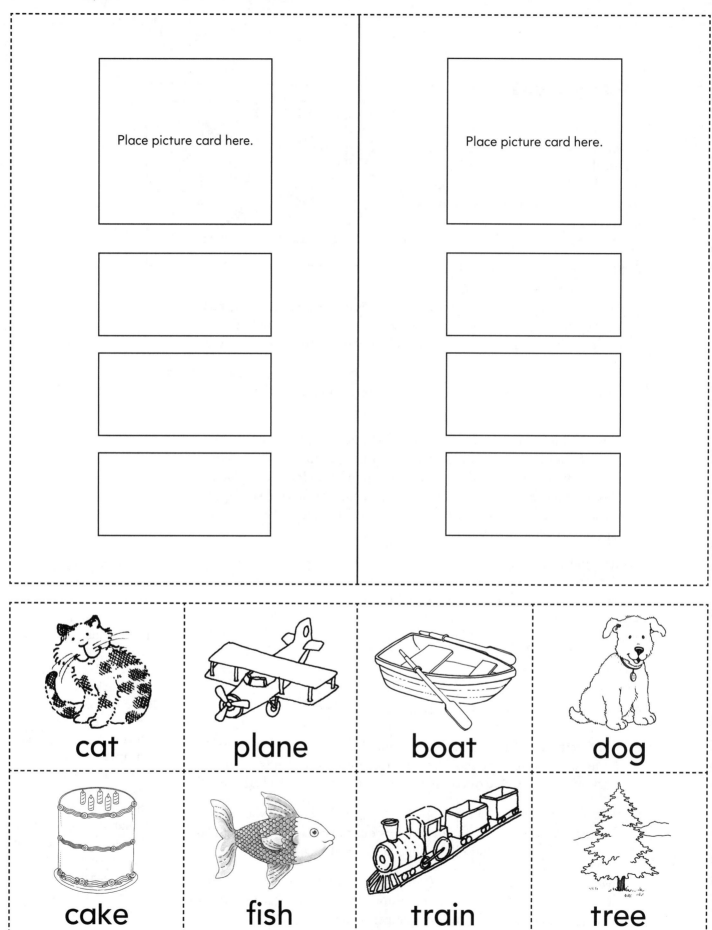

Place picture card here.

Place picture card here.

cat

plane

boat

dog

cake

fish

train

tree

cane	rat	scat	pat
coat	goat	crane	lane
frog	fog	log	float
wish	shake	bake	take
rain	main	swish	dish
three	bee	see	brain

Teaching Reading With Cynthia Rylant Books © 2009 by Joan Novelli, Scholastic Teaching Resources

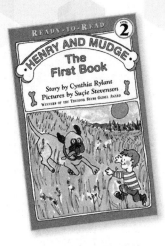

Henry and Mudge: The First Book

(SIMON & SCHUSTER, 1987)

"Henry had no brothers and no sisters." To make matters worse, there were no other children on his street. Henry's parents turn down his requests for a sibling or a move, and when he asks for a dog, they almost say "Sorry." But Henry's face is persuasive, and he soon has a new puppy to love. Mudge, of course, quickly grows to be the big dog Henry hoped for, and at three feet tall and 180 pounds, is often at the center of many unexpected and amusing situations. With characters that young readers can relate to, illustrations that support and extend the text, and plots that come to satisfying conclusions, the books in this celebrated series are just right for beginning readers.

> Use the suggestions on pages 72–76 with any Henry and Mudge book to support your reading program.

Before Reading

Children will quickly learn to read the words that begin each title: *Henry and Mudge*. As you preview the cover of a new book, invite children to read the title with you. Ask questions like the following to guide them in using the title and cover illustration to think about what they know and make predictions.

- Who do you see on the cover? Have you seen these characters before? What do you already know about them?
- How do words in the title match up with details in the picture?
- What do you think will happen with Henry and Mudge in this story? What are some clues?

During Reading

Whether they're playing in puddles or cracking codes, things happen when Henry and Mudge are around. Encourage children to join in on their adventures by teaching strategies for active reading.

- **"Listen" to Characters:** Mudge doesn't speak in these stories, but readers can learn a lot about this lovable dog from the illustrations. What do the expressions on his face say about what he is thinking or feeling? As you read, point out how the illustrations expand on what the text tells us.

- **Ask Questions:** Each book is divided into several chapters, providing an organization around which to ask questions and make predictions.

For example, in chapter 1 ("The Smart Dog") of *Henry and Mudge Take the Big Test*, children are left wondering, "How will Mudge do in dog school?" Based on what they know about Mudge, children may predict that dog school will have its ups and downs. And in chapter 2 ("School"), they'll find out if they're right!

☀ **Make Connections:** Children will naturally identify with Henry—for example, with his familiar fear of dogs that bite, thunderstorms, and nighttime noises, and also with his everyday adventures splashing in puddles, playing make-believe, and having sleepovers. Students will also connect with Henry as someone their age who has qualities much like their own. In *Henry and Mudge and the Careful Cousin*, for example, readers may find they are familiar with the situation under Henry's bed. Connections will come to mind from beginning to end, and using a "turn and talk" approach, in which children share their connections with a partner, will give everyone a chance to share.

After Reading

Guide a discussion that invites children to think about the story on different levels. The following suggestions are based on *Henry and Mudge: The First Book*, but can be adapted for use with other books in the series.

☀ **Recall Details:** Why did Henry want a dog? (*He doesn't have any brothers or sisters, and there are no other children on his street.*)

☀ **Make an Inference:** Why do you think Henry wanted a big dog? (For example, *a big dog can keep him safe.*)

☀ **Summarize:** What are the most important events in this story? (*Henry gets a dog; his dog gets lost; he finds his dog.*)

☀ **Explore Story Elements:** Why do you think the author decided to make Henry's friend a big dog, instead of, say, a small cat? (For example, *Henry will have different sorts of adventures with a big dog than he would with a small cat.*)

☀ **Evaluate:** Do you think Mudge is a good friend for Henry (or vice versa)? Why? Would you like to have a dog like Mudge (or a friend like Henry)? Why? (*Answers will vary.*)

More Adventures With Henry and Mudge

Titles in this popular series include:

- *Henry and Mudge: The First Book*
- *Henry and Mudge in Puddle Trouble*
- *Henry and Mudge in the Green Time*
- *Henry and Mudge Under the Yellow Moon*
- *Henry and Mudge in the Sparkle Days*
- *Henry and Mudge and the Forever Sea*
- *Henry and Mudge Get the Cold Shivers*
- *Henry and Mudge and the Happy Cat*
- *Henry and Mudge and the Bedtime Thumps*
- *Henry and Mudge Take the Big Test*
- *Henry and Mudge and the Long Weekend*
- *Henry and Mudge and the Wild Wind*
- *Henry and Mudge and the Careful Cousin*
- *Henry and Mudge and the Best Day of All*
- *Henry and Mudge in the Family Trees*
- *Henry and Mudge and the Sneaky Crackers*
- *Henry and Mudge and the Starry Night*
- *Henry and Mudge and Annie's Good Move*
- *Henry and Mudge and the Snowman Plan*
- *Henry and Mudge and Annie's Perfect Pet*
- *Henry and Mudge and the Tall Tree House*
- *Henry and Mudge and Mrs. Hopper's House*
- *Henry and Mudge and the Wild Goose Chase*
- *Henry and Mudge and the Funny Lunch*
- *Henry and Mudge and a Very Merry Christmas*
- *Henry and Mudge and the Great Grandpas*
- *Henry and Mudge and the Tumbling Trip*
- *Henry and Mudge and the Big Sleepover*

Tip

For more activities to use with the Henry and Mudge series, see Tips for Teaching With Chapter Books (pages 11–13).

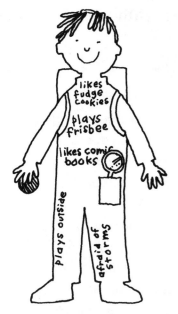

Book Buddies

Henry is just about the same age as his readers, making it easy for them to identify with him. Mudge is sure to become a beloved friend as well. Create life-size cutouts of this likable pair to link reading, writing, and art.

1. Revisit Henry and Mudge books and have children describe these two characters. List physical characteristics on chart paper.

2. Provide craft paper and other art supplies. Have children work together (perhaps having small groups take turns) to create life-size cutouts of Henry and Mudge. For Henry, they might trace around a classmate. For Mudge, they can begin by measuring and marking his height—three feet tall—and then draw an outline of a dog that size.

3. Encourage children to use art supplies to add features. For Henry, they might use orange yarn for his hair, glue on fabric-scrap pockets (which can hold something), and add construction-paper sneakers. Mudge will need a collar, a dog tag, and maybe a leash.

4. Display the cutouts and, as you read aloud books about Henry and Mudge, use them to record new information about these characters: their likes and dislikes, feelings, problems, and so on. Children will enjoy adding new items to the cutouts as they learn more about Henry and Mudge.

Pow! Boom!

Books in the Henry and Mudge series are sprinkled with words that help readers "hear" what's happening: "SPLASH!" as Mudge lands in a puddle (*Henry and Mudge in Puddle Trouble*); "FLOP!" as a moth in the dark sends Henry running for Mudge (*Henry and Mudge and the Bedtime Thumps*); "Whoosh!" as the wind "ripples" Mudge's fur (*Henry and Mudge and the Wild Wind*). Explore this poetic device with an activity that lets children express their understanding artistically.

1. Introduce the word *onomatopoeia*. Explain that this term refers to words that imitate sounds. Ask: "What sound does a dog make?" (*woof, ruff*) "What are some other words that name sounds?"

2. Hunt for examples of onomatopoeia in the books. (Often, these words appear in uppercase or italic letters, making them easy to spot.) Read the words aloud and list them on chart paper.

3. Give each child a sheet of paper. Have children choose a word from the list and draw a picture of it, using letter shapes, colors, and other details to create a "picture" of the word that matches the sound it represents.

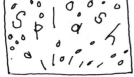

4. Display children's work. Point to each word and have children imitate the sound as they say the word. Encourage children to use the display as a reference to liven up their own writing.

Give the Dog a Bone

As a beginning-reader series, the Henry and Mudge books are designed to promote successful reading experiences. But students may encounter a few unfamiliar words. Explore new words to expand vocabulary and promote an "I can do it" attitude about reading more challenging material. These simple but effective games provide repeated practice with new words and let students see how their word knowledge is growing.

1. Make multiple copies of the dog and bone cards (page 76; enlarge first, if desired). Glue the pages to tagboard, then cut apart the cards.

2. As you read a story (or after reading), review unfamiliar words and their meanings. Write each word on a dog and a simple definition on a bone.

3. Use the word and definition cards to play the following games.

- **Here Doggie:** Give each child a dog or dog bone card. (Make sure each child can make a match.) Have children with the dog bones wander around the room calling "Here Doggie," as they look for the child whose dog makes a match with their bone. When a match is found, the pair says "Good Doggie" and sits down.

- **Woof:** Give each child a dog card. Read the definition on one bone at a time. When children hear the definition that matches their word, they call out "Woof" and take the bone.

- **Give the Dog a Bone:** Cover an empty cereal box with craft paper. Add a dog treat label (such as "Yummy Dog Treats"). Glue the dog cards around the outside of the box. Place a Velcro dot next to each dog. Affix a Velcro dot to the back of each bone, then put the bones in the box. Have children remove the bones and attach them next to the matching dogs.

Book Links

Young readers will delight in getting to know more fun friends in these beginning reader series.

- ☼ *Cowgirl Kate and Cocoa* by Erica Silverman (Harcourt, 2006): Whether they're counting cows or just keeping each other company, Kate and her horse Cocoa enjoy their days together.

- ☼ *Hi! Fly Guy* by Ted Arnold (Cartwheel, 2006): Buzz is looking for a special pet and finds what he's looking for in a fly that can say his name!

- ☼ *Iris and Walter* by Elissa Haden Guest (Harcourt, 2006): When Iris moves to the country, she misses her life in the city. But with her new friend, Walter, she soon discovers things to like about life in the country.

Tip

To help children make sense of the ways authors construct stories, play a game that invites them to consider how characters and events are connected. After sharing a Henry and Mudge story (or a chapter), pose a "What if?" question that asks children to look at an event from another angle—for example, "What if Henry's parents had said 'Sorry' to Henry when he asked for a dog?" After posing several "What if?" questions, let children give it a try. This exercise will help them recognize cause-and-effect relationships, and help them better understand why characters act, think, and feel as they do.

Teaching Reading With Cynthia Rylant Books © 2009 by Joan Novelli, Scholastic Teaching Resources

Activities for Teaching With More Books by Cynthia Rylant

Use the activities here to extend a read-aloud or as the basis for developing new lessons to add to a Cynthia Rylant author study.

This Year's Garden

(ATHENEUM, 1984)

Readers follow a young girl and her family through the seasons as they plan, plant, and harvest their garden. Illustrations by Mary Szilagyi may remind students of *Night in the Country* (see page 31), which she also illustrated. If desired, pair the books and compare the pictures to learn more about this illustrator's work.

Activity   A Year of Words

Reinforce concepts in the book by creating a colorful wall chart that features words related to each season.

1. Cut out a shape pattern to represent each season—for example, a sun for summer, a leaf for fall, a snowflake for winter, and a raindrop for spring.

2. Have children use the patterns to trace and cut out more copies of each. Divide mural paper into four sections and label each with the name of a season.

3. Fill a basket with the shape cutouts and markers or crayons.

4. Have children write words related to each season on the corresponding cutouts. Add the words to the wall chart to describe each season.

The Whales

(SCHOLASTIC/BLUE SKY PRESS, 1996)

Simple, poetic text celebrates whales, as they swim from one pole to the other, "floating like feathers in the deep blue green."

Activity   Unexpected Verbs

In *Wondrous Words*, Katie Wood Ray writes about "striking verbs," verbs that "catch a reader's attention." She explains, "Writers will choose verbs that readers don't expect to see with their subjects," and points to the first sentence of *The Whales* as an example.

1. Read the first sentence of the story, pausing just before the word *thinking*. Invite students to guess what word comes next—for example, *swimming, eating, diving, singing*, and *breaching* would all make sense.

2. Continue reading the sentence, then ask students why they think the author chose the word *thinking*. Do whales think? Do people think? Guide students to recognize that the author's use of the word *thinking* gives whales a human quality and invites readers to get to know the whales in an unexpected way—as creatures with friends and families, who sing, dream, love their children, and even have manners!

3. As you read the story, invite children to write down other unexpected or interesting words. Then let them share their words. Revisit those sections of the story and discuss the words students identified.

Tulip Sees America

(SCHOLASTIC, 1998)

A young man and his dog Tulip get in their little green car and set out from Ohio to see America. They see "farms like castles" in Iowa and feel the wind in Wyoming. They drive up mountains, across the desert, and out to Oregon's ocean where the water is "as far as you can see."

Activity More of America

Trace Tulip's route across America to learn more about the states he sees.

1. Have students use a map to trace Tulip's route from the beginning of the trip (Ohio) to the end (Oregon). Make a list of states the young man and his dog may have passed through but which are not mentioned in the book.

2. Invite student pairs to research one of these states and "add" a page to the story to tell what the characters might have seen.

3. Reread the book, inserting students' additions to the text along the way.

Long Night Moon

(SIMON & SCHUSTER, 2004)

As a woman and baby look out from their home on a moonlit night, readers see from their perspective the full moon from one month to the next. Graceful prose, set against shimmering nighttime scenes, introduces the names and qualities of the different full moons.

Activity Moons and Months

With a bit of research, children will discover that names given to full moons vary. For example, the "Stormy Moon" in *Long Night Moon* is also known as the "Wolf Moon" (Borland, 1979). Let children choose and research the name for a favorite full moon, such as for their birthday month, and use *Long Night Moon* as inspiration for writing and illustrating a poem about that moon. Guide children to notice the placement of the text on the pages of the book, a feature that they can try themselves.

All in a Day

(ABRAMS, 2009)

With rhythmic, rhyming text that reads like a poem, this story offers an inspiring message about filling up each day and making it count: "The day's all yours, it's waiting now. . . see what you can do." Striking cut-paper art may inspire readers' own artistic interpretations of what a day brings.

Activity Today's the Day

Use the story as inspiration for setting class goals. Setting goals helps children develop self-direction in their learning and gain confidence in their abilities. Invite children to help set a class goal for the day with this morning message activity.

1. As part of the day's morning message, state a goal you have for the day, such as to have time to share a new book. Close the message by inviting children to suggest another class goal for the day. Place sticky notes at the morning message easel for students' responses.

2. When children arrive at school, have them read the message, take a sticky note to their seat, write a response, then stick the note to the message pad (below the message).

3. Bring children together to discuss ideas and decide on a class goal for the day. Have them suggest ways to accomplish the goal, then get started on a great day! To go further, encourage children to set personal learning goals for the day (or week).

A Cynthia Rylant Celebration: Culminating Activities

Wrap up your Cynthia Rylant author study with activities that invite students to revisit important themes and characters, make connections to their own lives, and reflect on what they like best about this author's books.

From *When I Was Young in the Mountains* to *Poppleton*, books by Cynthia Rylant are wide-ranging, but they share qualities that make them recognizably hers. Invite students to think back about the books they've read. If possible, have each title available to revisit. Use the questions here to guide a discussion that lets students share what they've learned.

☼ What different kinds of books does Cynthia Rylant write? (for example, *picture books and chapter books*) What do you like about each?

☼ Are the characters (or places) in her books alike in any way? How?

☼ What kinds of books do you think Cynthia Rylant likes to write?

☼ What's fun about Cynthia Rylant's books for you as a reader?

☼ How do these books make you think of something you'd like to try in your own writing?

Guess Who?

Play a fast-paced game that strengthens use of descriptive vocabulary as children look back on characters they've gotten to know.

1. Write characters' names on slips of paper and place them in a bag or hat.

2. Let children take turns selecting a character and giving descriptions one by one until someone guesses the correct character. The goal of the student providing descriptions is to keep the list going as long as possible (so a strategy might be to share the tiniest of details). The goal of the class is to guess the character as soon as possible.

Friendship Stories

Friendship is a recurring theme in books by Cynthia Rylant. Weave this theme into a culminating activity that also celebrates the special friendships in students' own lives.

1. Revisit special friendships in books by Cynthia Rylant, such as those portrayed in *The Relatives Came*, *The Old Woman Who Named Things*, *The Bookshop Dog*, and *Miss Maggie*.

2. Discuss reasons a theme such as "friendship" might pop up in different books by the same author. For example, the author might want to inspire readers to appreciate important people in their own lives.

3. Celebrate classroom friendships by making and exchanging simple friendship bracelets. Give

(continued)

each child four equal lengths of embroidery thread in different colors, measuring approximately the length of a child's arm. Have children knot the threads together at one end. Pair up children and have them follow these steps to make each bracelet:

- One person holds the knotted end of the strings tightly, while a partner twists the other end until the entire length is tightly twisted.

- Tie a double knot at the other end.

- To wear, push one of the knotted ends through the twisted threads at the other end.

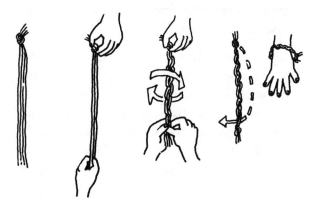

4. As students make their bracelets, encourage them to share favorite stories about friendship with each other. Have children exchange bracelets with their partners.

And the Award Goes to...

Cynthia Rylant's books have won many awards, including a Caldecott Honor for *When I Was Young in the Mountains* and for *The Relatives Came*. What award would students give this author's books? As students think about

the answer, they'll summarize, analyze, and reflect on what they have learned about the author's work. This activity also gives students a chance to incorporate art (designing an award or medal) and public speaking (presenting the award).

1. Students may be familiar with the Caldecott Medal and Honor awards. Share the cover of *When I Was Young in the Mountains* or *The Relatives Came* and let children take a closer look at the award sticker. (You can also view pictures of a Caldecott medal online at the Association for Library Service to Children Web site: www.ala.org/ala/mgrps/divs/alsc/.) Take a moment to share with children the history behind this award: The Caldecott medal, named for a children's illustrator, was first awarded in 1937 and is given each year in honor of the best illustrations in a picture book. The medal is made of bronze and engraved (on the back) with the winner's name and date of the award.

2. Invite students to pair up to create an award for a favorite Cynthia Rylant book. (In advance, inquire about students' favorite books and pair them accordingly.)

3. Provide time for students to discuss the books and decide on an appropriate award. Have them create a tangible symbol of the award (they might use the Caldecott medal as inspiration) and share a brief presentation that includes their reasons for the recognition.

Tip

As children prepare to present their awards, take time to reinforce characteristics of good speaking and listening skills. Consider displaying the awards in the library as part of a Cynthia Rylant display to inspire others to get to know this favorite author.